Computing Fundamentals Concepts

3rd Edition

William S. Davis

Miami University, Oxford, Ohio

 Addison-Wesley Publishing Company

Reading, Massachusetts · Menlo Park, California · New York
Don Mills, Ontario · Wokingham, England · Amsterdam ·
Bonn · Sydney · Singapore · Tokyo · Madrid · San Juan

This book was produced by the Addison-Wesley Electronic Production Department on an Apple Macintosh II with PageMaker. The output was generated on an Apple LaserWriter II NTX.

This book is in the Addison-Wesley *Computing Fundamentals Series*.

Series Editor: William S. Davis

Library of Congress Cataloging-in-Publication Data
Davis, William S., 1943-
    Computing fundamentals : concepts / William S. Davis.—3rd ed.
        p.   cm.
    Includes index.
    ISBN 0-201-52746-4
    1. Computers. 2. Electronic data processing. I. Title.
QA76.D3333155   1991
004—dc20   90-45499
                                                        CIP

3 4 5 6 7 8 9 10 MA 95 94 93 92 91

The Computing Fundamentals Series

The books in Addison-Wesley's *Computing Fundamentals Series* feature tutorials that teach the reader how to use specific software packages. Their low selling price makes them attractive as self-teaching aids and as supplements to a primary text. A unique feature entitled "What can go wrong?" anticipates problems, suggests a cause, and helps the reader recover. The modular nature of the series should prove attractive to the instructor of a microcomputer applications course. Current and planned titles include:

dBASE III PLUS™
dBASE IV™
Excel™ *for the Macintosh*®
Lotus® *1-2-3*® *Release 2.01/2.2*
Microsoft® *Word for the IBM PC*
Microsoft® *Word for the Macintosh*®

PageMaker® *for the IBM PC*
PageMaker® *for the Macintosh*®
PC-DOS & MS-DOS®
UNIX®
WordPerfect 5.0/5.1®

Preface

The first edition of this book was published in 1986 under the title *Fundamental Computer Concepts*. The *Computing Fundamentals Series* was created in 1989, and a second edition, retitled simply *Concepts*, became part of that series. Technology has changed over the past two years. Add the advice, suggestions, and observations of the second edition's adopters and readers, and the time has come for a third edition.

Because the book emphasizes *fundamental* concepts, relatively few major changes were required. At the request of several users, a brief overview of computer evolution has been added to Chapter 1, more details about OS/2, Windows, and UNIX have been integrated into Chapter 6, and an introduction to the program development process now appears in Chapter 7, Additionally, the coverage of application software has been revised, and Chapter 11 has been rewritten to reflect more accurately the state of the art in data communication. Finally, a new Chapter 12 discusses typical computer system configurations and explains how the computing environment influences applications. Other, less substantial, changes appear throughout the book.

Like the first two editions, *Computing Fundamentals: Concepts* is an inexpensive, technically accurate, easy-to-read introduction to those concepts that are fundamental to understanding computers. It can be used alone, in conjunction with outside readings, or as a supplement to a programming or computer application text. The other books in Addison-Wesley's *Computing Fundamentals Series* teach specific computer-related skills. They, too, can be used alone or as supplements to a primary text. Combined with this text, they can also be used to support a microcomputer application course.

Acknowledgments

The third edition owes much to the people who helped create the first two, including: Venis Torge, Dr. Allison McCormack, Mark Dalton, Katherine Harutunian, Mark Coffee, Joyce Snow, Keith Wollman, Deborah Lafferty, and a host of reviewers. I owe a special thanks to my students and colleagues at Miami University for many valuable suggestions. Additionally, numerous comments and suggestions from second edition adopters proved invaluable. Finally, I would like to acknowledge the third edition reviewers: Dr. Bruce Brown of Salt Lake Community College, Paul Hanna of Florida State University, Carol Jeffries of the University of North Carolina, and Gail Leslie of Stephen Austin State University.

Contents

Contents

Contents   xi

Computers: Getting Started

Preview

A modern computer is composed of numerous components. Keeping track of all those components can sometimes be confusing to a beginner. The purpose of this first chapter is to set the stage for the chapters that follow by giving you a sense of what computers do. Key concepts include:

What is a computer?

- Data and information
- Data processing
- The stored program concept

The evolution of computing technology

- Before computers
- The first computers
- First-, second-, and third-generation machines
- The microcomputer revolution
- The future

A computer system

- System components

- The input/process/output cycle

- Hardware and software

Succeeding chapters will discuss each of the computer's components in more detail. As you read them, think of the material in this chapter as a road map that helps you see each component in context.

What Is a Computer?

Data and Information

A medieval astronomer named Tycho Brahe spent his entire adult life observing and recording the positions of the planets. His successor, Johannes Kepler, sensed a pattern in those observations, and spent much of his life processing them, performing tedious computations in an attempt to verify the pattern. Eventually, he succeeded, publishing his laws of planetary motion in 1621.

Tycho Brahe collected **data**, raw facts. Kepler's laws represent **information**. Using them, he could understand and predict the motions of the planets. Using them, modern scientists and engineers plan space flights. Information has meaning.

Clearly, Kepler's laws were derived from Brahe's data, but the raw data were useless without processing. Until they were organized and the necessary calculations performed, the data were just unstructured facts, with no clear meaning. Knowing the exact position of Mars on April 1, 1599 might earn an extra move in Trivial Pursuit, but by itself that fact is not very useful. Processing data extracts their meaning.

Data Processing

A computer is a **data processing** machine. Data flow into the machine as **input** (Fig. 1.1). Information flows from the machine as **output**. The computer processes the data. Its primary advantages are speed and accuracy.

The word "process" implies that a change takes place, that the raw materials are in some way restructured or manipulated. A computer processes data by filtering and summarizing them so that underlying patterns can be perceived. Generally, computers can add, subtract, multiply, divide, compare, copy, start input, and start output. So can most calculators. What makes a computer different?

The Stored Program Concept

To add two numbers on a calculator, you:

1. Enter the first number.

2. Press the add (+) button.

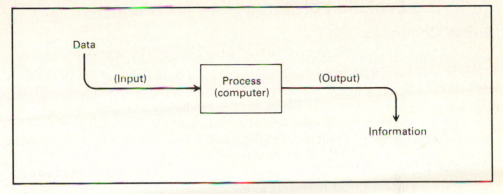

Figure 1.1 A computer is a machine that processes data into information. It accepts data, processes the data, and generates information as output.

3. Enter the second number.

4. Press the result (=) button.

5. Record the sum for future reference.

The calculator finds the sum, but *you* provide control by deciding what button to push next. A calculator requires direct human intervention at each step.

A computer processes data automatically, with no need for human intervention. Computers are *not* intelligent, however. They cannot decide independently when to add, subtract, compare, or request input. If a computer is to function without direct human control, it must be given a set of instructions called a **program** to guide it. The program is physically stored inside the machine, making it a **stored program** (Fig. 1.2). The stored program distinguishes a computer from a calculator and allows it to function without human intervention. Thus a **computer** can be defined as *a machine that processes data into information under the control of a stored program.*

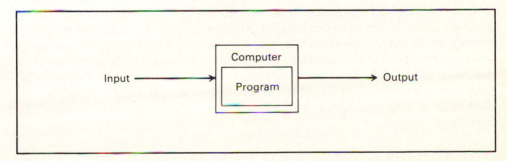

Figure 1.2 A computer processes data automatically under control of a stored program.

Computers: Getting Started
What Is a Computer?

The Evolution of Computing Technology

Before Computers

Johannes Kepler spent a lifetime performing calculations to prove his laws of planetary motion. Today, a college student with a computer can verify those calculations in a few hours. Kepler certainly could have used a computer, but the technology of his time was not capable of producing one, and, except for a handful of scientists, few people needed such a machine. Technological change requires both adequate technology *and* a perceived need. Both conditions were missing in 1691, so computers did not exist.

The first aids to computation appeared thousands of years ago when our ancestors progressed from bartering to money-based economies. Early merchants had a need to record and track business transactions accurately. That need, in turn, led to such inventions as the abacus (Fig. 1.3), the Roman counting board, and ledger books (or scrolls). The technology was rather primitive, but given the nature of the need it was good enough.

By the early 1600s, international trade had become big business, and merchant ships sailed all over the world. One problem was the available navigational tables. They were prepared manually and contained numerous errors that resulted in the loss of many ships. Inspired in part by this need, John Napier invented logarithms and a primitive slide rule in 1617, Blaise Pascal created an adding machine in 1647, and Gottfried Wilhelm Liebnitz built a machine capable of multiplication in 1673 (Fig. 1.3). Their ideas were good, but fifteenth century technology was incapable of working to the necessary precision. A need existed, but because technology was lacking their inventions had little immediate impact.

The industrial revolution of the 1800s brought both an increased need for data processing and rapidly evolving technology. Technological change tends to feed on itself. For example, in 1806 Joseph Jacquard invented an automated weaving machine controlled by punched cards. Later in that century, his idea was borrowed by Herman Hollerith, who had the data from the 1890 United States census recorded on punched cards and used newly developed electronic machines to process the counts. His inventions spawned a punched card industry that dominated business data processing well into the 1950s.

Charles Babbage was not quite as successful. By 1843 he had drawn up detailed plans for an analytical engine, a machine that incorporated virtually every component and function of a modern computer. Unfortunately, no one was interested, and the technology of his time was not capable of building his machine, so his idea died. In fact, were it not for the writings of Ada Augusta, Countess of Lovelace (the daughter of the British poet Byron), Babbage's contribution to the evolution of computing technology might have been lost to history.

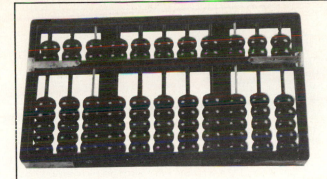

ABACUS
c. 1200 ("Suan-pan") China

Calculator of antiquity that historians trace vaguely to Egypt, India, and Mesopotamia

NAPIER'S RODS

1617   John Napier   Scotland

Mathematician and co-inventor of logarithms, Napier devised these computing rods to simplify multiplication. They were widely used during the seventeenth century.

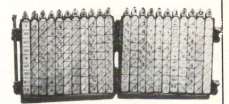

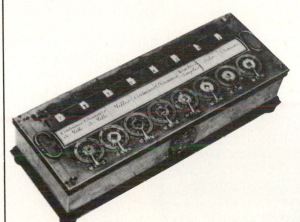

MACHINE ARITHMETIQUE
1647–1653   Blaise Pascal   France

The first real calculating machine. The stylus-operated figure wheels are so geared that a complete revolution of any wheel advances the wheel to the left of it one number. It is limited to addition and subtraction.

Figure 1.3 Some early aids to computation. (Reprinted by permission of the Fine Arts Department of the International Business Machines Corporation.)

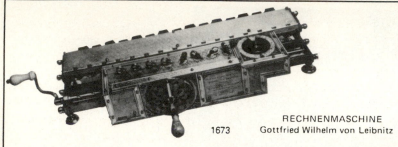

RECHNENMASCHINE

1673   Gottfried Wilhelm von Leibnitz   Germany

Designed to perform multiplication by rapidly repeated
addition. The mechanism was not completely reliable,
but the "stepped reckoner" principle that Leibnitz devised
was used in the Thomas and other calculators.

POCKET CALCULATOR

C. 1800   France
Combination of Chinese abacus
and mechanized Napier's rods.

ARITHMOMETER

1820   Thomas de Colmar   France

This first commercially practical calculating machine used
the Leibnitz "stepped reckoner" principle. Its manufacture
was made possible by the new production methods of
the Industrial Revolution.

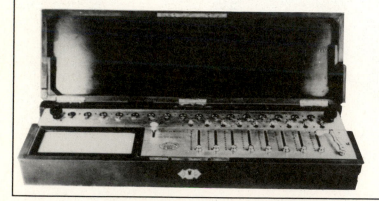

Figure 1.3 (Continued)

The First Computers

Throughout the first half of the twentieth century, punched card equipment represented the state of the data processing art. However, the pressures of two world wars and developments in the physical sciences rapidly created both new needs and new knowledge. In 1939, Howard Aiken of Harvard University began working on a machine to help solve polynomials; his Mark I, the very first electromechanical computer, was finished in 1944. One of his assistants, a young U.S. Navy lieutenant named Grace M. Hopper, would later become the creator of the business programming language, COBOL.

Even more important was the work conducted at the University of Pennsylvania under the direction of John W. Mauchly and J. Presper Eckert. Ready in 1945, two months after the surrender of Japan, their machine, the ENIAC (Fig. 1.4), is widely recognized as the world's first electronic computer. Some experts believe that Mauchly and Eckert were influenced by an earlier model developed by John V. Atanasoff of Iowa State College. Others point to once-secret machines created in both England and Germany during World War II. Still, there is no denying that the ENIAC was the machine that started the computer age.

Figure 1.4 The ENIAC. (Photograph courtesy of The Moore School of Electrical Engineering, University of Pennsylvania.)

First-, Second-, and Third-Generation Machines

Mauchly and Eckert left the university, founded a corporation to manufacture computers, and, in 1951, sold a machine named the UNIVAC I to the U.S. Census Bureau. Soon, other firms began marketing computers, and a new industry was born. Compared to today's machines, these **first-generation** computers were rather primitive. Their key components, electronic tubes, tended to burn out quickly, and that created reliability problems. The machines were massive, consumed a great deal of power, and needed a virtual army of operators and programmers to attend them.

Then came the invention of the transistor and the development of **second-generation** computers. Compared to tubes, transistors were smaller, less expensive, and much more reliable, and by 1960 electronic tube machines were virtually obsolete. By the mid-1960s second-generation computers had, in turn, been supplanted by smaller, faster, more powerful, more reliable, less expensive **third-generation** machines that used integrated circuit technology (Fig. 1.5).

The Microcomputer Revolution

In 1971, Intel Corporation announced the first microprocessor, in effect a complete computer on a chip about the size of your fingernail. By 1975,

Figure 1.5 First-generation tubes, second-generation transistors, and third-generation integrated circuits. (Photograph courtesy of International Business Machines Corporation.)

personal computers appeared; and a few years later, Apple, Radio Shack, and several other firms were actively selling them. The **microcomputer** revolution had begun.

Initially, microcomputers were sold almost exclusively to hobbyists. Then, in 1979, a program called Visicalc appeared. It allowed business people to create and manipulate spreadsheets on an Apple computer. Given an application that met a real need, microcomputer sales boomed. A few years later, the IBM Personal Computer was announced, and sophisticated word processing and database programs began to appear.

Unfortunately, if two accountants independently prepare the same spreadsheet from even slightly different data, the results can be quite different. There are advantages to having everyone access the same data. The solution is to link several microcomputers to a centralized computer over a network. Interconnected computers accessing a common database is the current state of the art in computer technology.

The Future

Predicting the future is always risky, but one good clue is to study current research. For example, research centers in Europe, the United States, and Japan are actively studying artificial intelligence (AI), and some experts believe that artificially intelligent machines will characterize computing's fifth generation.

Artificial intelligence research is focused in three main areas. Natural language processing is concerned with the way people communicate with computers. Today, we still must translate our needs into computer terms; tomorrow, the computer might be able to understand us. Expert systems attempt to simulate the decision-making process of a human expert, and several interesting applications have already been successfully tested. Robotics is concerned with developing robots that simulate various human capabilities. Look for features derived from this research to appear soon.

In any event, tomorrow's computers will almost certainly be more powerful, smaller, more reliable, less expensive, and easier to use than today's. Change may well be the only constant in the computer field. If the recent past is any indication, the future promises to be very interesting.

A Computer System

System Components

A modern computer system consists of several basic components (Fig. 1.6). An input device provides data. The data are stored in **memory**, which also holds a program. Under control of the program, the computer's **processor** manipulates the data, storing the results back into memory. Finally, the results flow from the computer to an output device. Additionally, most modern computers use secondary storage to extend memory capacity.

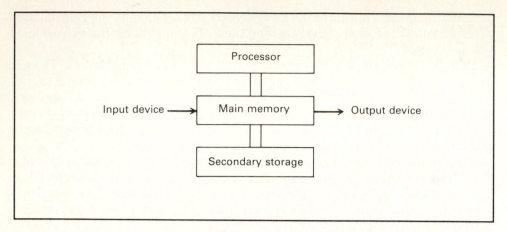

Figure 1.6 A computer system consists of four basic components: an input device, an output device, memory, and a processor. Secondary storage is often used to extend memory capacity.

Consider the computer system pictured in Fig. 1.7. The keyboard is an input device; the display screen is an output device. The image displayed on a screen is temporary; a more permanent copy of the output can be obtained by

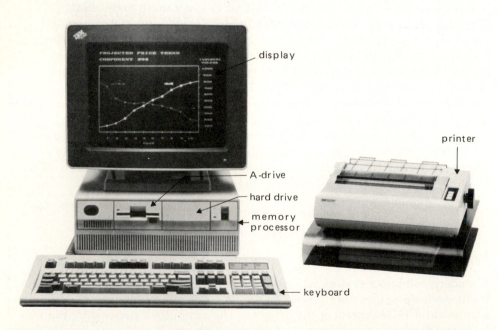

Figure 1.7 A typical computer system. Input is provided by a keyboard. Output goes to the screen or to the printer. The processor and main memory are located inside the cabinet. The disk drives provide secondary storage. Courtesy of International Business Machines Corporation.

sending it to a printer. The computer's processor and memory are located inside the cabinet. The diskette drives extend the computer's memory; programs often enter the system through such secondary storage devices.

The Input/Process/Output Cycle

The first step in using a computer is to store a program in memory (Fig. 1.8a). Given a program, the processor can begin processing data. Input data from the keyboard are stored in memory (Fig. 1.8b). The processor manipulates the data, storing the results back into memory (Fig. 1.8c). Finally, the results are output (Fig. 1.8d). This input/process/output pattern is common to most computer applications.

Hardware and Software

Because memory's contents are easy to change, when one set of data has been processed, the program can be repeated, reading and processing new data

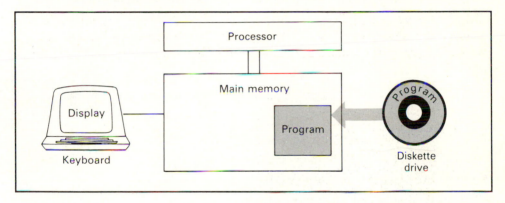

Figure 1.8(a) The first step in using a computer is to store a program in memory.

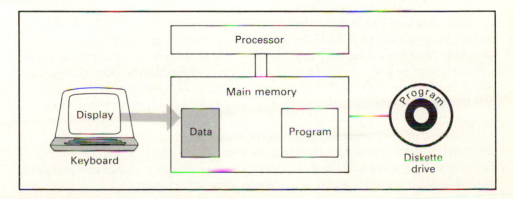

Figure 1.8(b) Under control of the stored program, data are read from the keyboard and stored in memory.

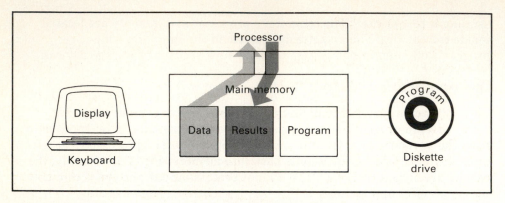

Figure 1.8(c) The processor manipulates the data, storing the results back in memory.

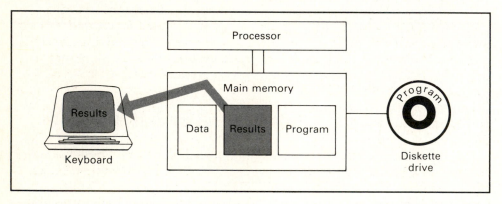

Figure 1.8(d) Finally, the results are output.

and generating new output. If the data can be changed, why not the program? When a program is finished, a new one can take its place in memory, allowing the computer to process completely different data. One minute the computer can generate paychecks from labor data under control of a payroll program. The next minute, it can prepare bills from invoices under control of a billing program. Later, this same collection of components, controlled by yet another program, can read statistical data and produce a bar chart or sense the movements of a joystick and manipulate the position of an imaginary spaceship on a display screen.

A computer's physical components—the processor, memory, input devices, and output devices—are its **hardware**. You can see them, touch them, and feel them. Programs and data are different, existing only as electronic pulses stored in memory. **Software** is a general term for programs.

A Plan of Attack

At this point, you should have a basic sense of the functions performed by the processor, main memory, input devices, output devices, and secondary storage; and you should know that a computer processes data under the control of a program. Over the next several chapters, you'll study each major component in more detail, beginning with the computer itself. Later, you'll consider how the components are assembled to form complete computer systems.

As you study the processor, or memory, or input devices, or software, it's easy to become bogged down in technical details and thus to "miss the forest for the trees." Don't lose sight of the fact that a computer is a collection of components, each of which must do its part.

Summary

A computer is a machine that processes data into information under the control of a stored program. Although the need for data processing has existed since prehistoric times, the first computers did not appear until shortly after World War II. First-generation computers relied on electronic tubes. By 1960, they had been supplanted by transistorized second-generation machines. By the middle 1960s, modern integrated circuits ushered in a third generation, and improved integrated circuits made the microcomputer revolution of the mid-1970s possible. Many experts believe that artificial intelligence will characterize computing's fifth generation.

Data enter a computer through an input device, are stored in memory and manipulated by the processor, and the results are sent to an output device. Many computers use secondary storage to extend memory capacity. A computer's physical components are called hardware. Software is a general term for programs. The chapter ended with a brief overview of the rest of the text.

Key Words

At the end of each chapter, you'll find a list of key words. You should know what these terms mean; if you don't, reread the material. After defining each term in your own words, check your answers against the glossary.

computer	input	program
data	memory	second generation
data processing	microcomputer	software
first generation	output	stored program
hardware	processor	third generation
information		

Self-Test

At the end of each chapter you'll find a brief self-test; the answers are in Appendix B. Use the questions to check your understanding of key terms and concepts. If you miss a question, review the associated material. If you miss several, reread the chapter.

1. Unstructured facts are called _data_. Processing data yields _information_, which has meaning.
2. A computer processes _data_ into _information_.
3. Data flow into the computer as _input_. Information flows from the computer as _output_.
4. The _stored program_ distinguishes a computer from a calculator.
5. The first electronic computer, the _ENIAC_, was developed by Eckert and Mauchly in 1945.
6. The primary component of a first-generation computer was an electronic _tube_. Second-generation machines used _transistor_, and third-generation computers used modern _integrated circuit_.
7. Many experts believe that fifth-generation computers will have _Artificial intelligence_.
8. Data and program instructions are stored in _memory_. The computer component that actually manipulates the data is the _processor_.
9. The physical components of a computer are collectively called _hardware_.
10. Programs are known collectively as _software_.

Relating the Concepts

Because there is more to understanding computer concepts than knowing the meanings of a few terms, each chapter ends with a set of subjective questions. Some will ask you to explain a concept, explain why a computer works as it does, relate concepts, or link concepts presented in two or more chapters. A few will ask you to extrapolate from the material presented in this book. No answers are suggested.

1. Distinguish between data and information.
2. Relate the terms *data* and *information* to the terms *input* and *output*.
3. A stored program distinguishes a computer from a calculator. Explain.
4. What is a computer? Don't just reproduce the definition; explain what each technical term in the definition means.
5. Briefly distinguish between first-, second-, and third-generation computers.
6. Two conditions are necessary for technological development: a need and existing technology. Briefly explain why.

7. Draw a sketch showing the primary components of a typical computer system. Briefly explain what each component does.

8. Explain the difference between hardware and software.

9. Briefly explain a computer's basic input/process/output cycle.

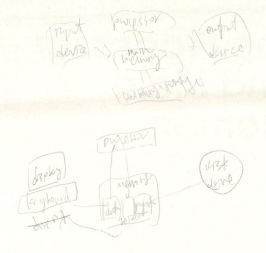

2

The Processor and Main Memory

Preview

This chapter takes you inside the computer and explains how each of the major internal components works. Key concepts include:

The binary number system

Main memory

- Physical storage devices

- Bytes and words

- Addressing memory

- Reading and writing memory

The processor

- Instructions

- Processor components

- Machine cycles

The Binary Number System

If you take the cover off a small computer and look inside (Fig. 2.1), you'll see a few circuit boards, some cables, and some wires. The real computer lies within the circuitry on those boards. This chapter will zero in for a closer look. First, however, consider the "language" of a computer: **binary**.

A computer operates on precisely timed pulses of electric current. The processor reacts to pulse and no-pulse patterns. Memory holds these on/off patterns. The binary number system is ideal for representing such patterns because it uses only two symbols: 0 and 1.

Generally, a number system is a scheme for representing numeric values. The decimal number system uses combinations of ten symbols, 0 through 9. The digits alone are not enough, however; their relative positions are also important. For example, you know that 03 is three and 30 is thirty because of the digit 3's relative position. Each position has a value. The positional values (1, 10, 100, 1000) are factors of ten. The value of a number is determined by multiplying each digit by its positional value and then adding the products (Fig. 2.2).

In the binary number system the positional values are factors of 2: 1, 2, 4, 8, 16, ... (Fig. 2.3). Only two symbols are needed: 0 and 1. The "digit-times-place-value" rule still holds, however; to find the value of any number,

Figure 2.1 Inside a typical microcomputer. Courtesy of International Business Machines Corporation.

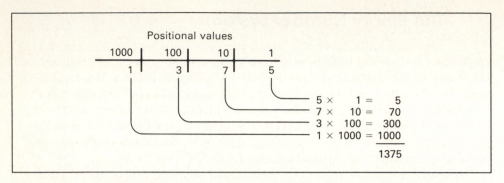

Figure 2.2 In the decimal number system, positional values are factors of ten. To find the value of any number, multiply each digit by its positional value and add the products.

multiply each digit by its place or positional value and add the products. Thus, as you can see in Fig. 2.3, the binary number 10 is equivalent to the decimal number 2, while 101 is equivalent to the decimal number 5.

We use decimal numbers because we find them convenient (probably because we have ten fingers). A computer uses binary numbers because its structure makes binary convenient. A binary digit, or **bit**, is the computer's basic unit of storage. Physical storage devices hold bits. Processors manipulate bits. A computer is a binary machine.

For most readers a basic sense of the binary number system is enough. Others, particularly students who plan to major in a computer-related discipline, might require more depth. Appendix A presents additional details on number systems, data formats, and codes.

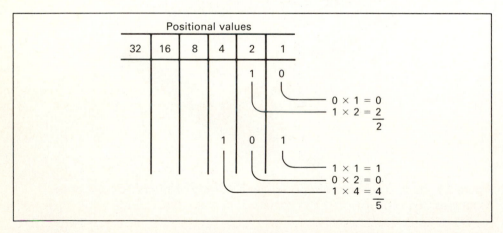

Figure 2.3 In the binary number system, positional values are factors of two. The "digit-times-place-value" rule still works.

Main Memory

Physical Storage Devices

Consider the bank of switches and light bulbs pictured in Fig. 2.4. Each switch is a simple mechanical device that can assume either of two states: on or off. Note the switch settings. If you supply an electric current, which bulbs will light? Obviously, only those controlled by the switches set on. If you repeat the experiment, the same bulbs will light. If you change the switch settings, different bulbs will light. The switch is a primitive storage or memory device in which "on" represents a 1-bit and "off" a 0-bit.

Carefully distinguish between the physical device (the switch) and its value (0 or 1). The switch is hardware; its *setting* represents software or data. The value is easy to change—just flip the switch. The value (the software or data) is not permanent; the hardware (the switch) is.

Any device that can assume and hold either of two states is a potential memory device, but most modern computers use **random access memory (RAM)** integrated circuit chips (Fig. 2.5). Each chip can store hundreds of thousands of bits. A small computer might contain a few dozen chips; a large machine might contain thousands. The difference is one of degree, not function.

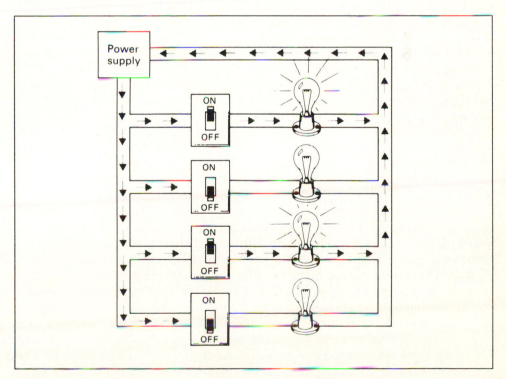

Figure 2.4 A light switch is a simple example of a storage or memory device.

Figure 2.5 The memory of a modern computer is composed of random access memory (RAM) chips. Photo courtesy of Motorola, Inc.

Bytes and Words

A single bit can hold either a 0 or a 1. Generally, however, the contents of memory are envisioned as groups of bits rather than as individual bits, for the same reasons that we focus on words and sentences rather than individual letters when we read a novel. Although the bit is still the basic unit of storage, computers normally manipulate bytes or words.

A **byte** contains enough bits (usually eight) to represent a single character. Two binary codes, ASCII (the American Standard Code for Information Interchange) and EBCDIC (the Extended Binary Coded Decimal Interchange Code), are commonly used to represent characters inside a computer (Fig. 2.6). Each byte can hold a single letter, digit, or punctuation mark.

Bytes are fine for storing characters but are too small to hold a meaningful number. Most computers are able to manipulate a group of bytes called a **word**. Some small computers have 8-bit words. Other, more powerful machines work with 16-bit (2-byte), 32-bit (4-byte), and even 64-bit words.

The basic unit of storage is the bit. Bits are grouped to form bytes, which in turn are grouped to form words (Fig. 2.7). In one application a given word might be used to hold a binary number. In another, that word's bytes might hold individual characters, or a program instruction.

It is important to note that character data and numeric data are different. Characters are represented by a code, and each character is independent. The concept of positional value is irrelevant; multiplying each bit in the code by its positional value and then adding the products produces a meaningless result. In contrast, the bits that form a number are coded in specific relative

Character	EBCDIC	ASCII-8
A	1100 0001	1010 0001
B	1100 0010	1010 0010
C	1100 0011	1010 0011
D	1100 0100	1010 0100
E	1100 0101	1010 0101
F	1100 0110	1010 0110
G	1100 0111	1010 0111
H	1100 1000	1010 1000
I	1100 1001	1010 1001
J	1101 0001	1010 1010
K	1101 0010	1010 1011
L	1101 0011	1010 1100
M	1101 0100	1010 1101
N	1101 0101	1010 1110
O	1101 0110	1010 1111
P	1101 0111	1011 0000
Q	1101 1000	1011 0001
R	1101 1001	1011 0010
S	1110 0010	1011 0011
T	1110 0011	1011 0100
U	1110 0100	1011 0101
V	1110 0101	1011 0110
W	1110 0110	1011 0111
X	1110 0111	1011 1000
Y	1110 1000	1011 1001
Z	1110 1001	1011 1010
0	1111 0000	0101 0000
1	1111 0001	0101 0001
2	1111 0010	0101 0010
3	1111 0011	0101 0011
4	1111 0100	0101 0100
5	1111 0101	0101 0101
6	1111 0110	0101 0110
7	1111 0111	0101 0111
8	1111 1000	0101 1000
9	1111 1001	0101 1001

Figure 2.6 The ASCII and EBCDIC codes are often used to represent characters inside a computer.

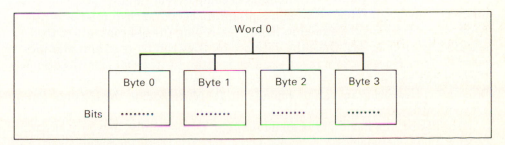

Figure 2.7 In a computer's memory, bits are combined to form bytes, and bytes in turn are combined to form words. This example pictures a 32-bit or 4-byte word.

positions, each of which has a positional value: 1, 2, 4, 8, and so on. The "digit-times-place-value" rule works with numbers but not with characters. (See Appendix A for more detail.)

Addressing Memory

A typical microcomputer has at least 512KB (kilobytes, or thousands of bytes) of storage capacity; a large computer might contain several megabytes (millions of bytes) or even gigabytes (billions of bytes). A given element of data might be stored in any one of them. If the processor needs a particular data element, how does it find the byte that holds it?

Each physical storage unit is assigned a unique **address**. On most computers the bytes or words are numbered sequentially—0, 1, 2, and so on. The processor accesses a specific memory location by referencing its address. For example, if the processor needs the data stored in byte 1048, it asks memory for the contents of byte 1048. Since there is only one byte 1048, the processor gets the right data. Depending on the computer, bytes or words are the basic addressable units of memory. Data move between the processor and memory a byte or a word at a time.

Reading and Writing Memory

A location in **main memory** is accessed by its address. When memory is read, its contents are not changed. For example, imagine that byte number 42 contains the character A. If the processor reads byte 42, the A is still there. However, writing to main memory destroys the old contents. If the processor were to write the character X to byte 42, the new value would replace the old one, and the A would disappear.

Consider the distinction between reading and writing memory from a slightly different perspective, because it is potentially confusing. On input, data are read from an input device and written to memory. On output, data are read from memory and written to an output device. In each case, note that the term "read" refers to the source of the data, while "write" refers to their destination.

The main memory of most computers is composed of random access memory. The programmer (through a program, of course) can read or write RAM. Input data can be stored in RAM, destroying the old contents of the selected bytes or words. Once the data are in, they can be read and manipulated by the processor, and results can be written to other memory locations. Finally, the contents can be sent to an output device. When a program is finished, a new program can be copied into RAM, replacing the old one. The contents of RAM are easy to change.

Usually, RAM's flexibility is an advantage. Occasionally, however, it can be a problem. Consider, for example, the automatic teller terminals used in many banks. They are controlled by small computers, which in turn are controlled by programs. A sharp programmer might be able to modify one of those programs to give free access to certain accounts. Needless to say, the bank could not tolerate such changes. The bank needs a program that can be read by the processor but not modified. Such programs are stored in **read-only memory (ROM)**. Another good example of a ROM-based program is the BASIC language interpreter found in many microcomputers; you'll learn about interpreters in Chapter 7. As the name implies, ROM is "permanent" memory that can be read but not written.

Think of RAM as a scratch pad that holds current programs and current data; its contents can be changed in a tiny fraction of a second. In contrast, ROM is permanent and cannot be easily changed. RAM is the computer's general-purpose memory. ROM is used for a few key program modules.

The Processor

The **processor**, often called the **central processing unit (CPU)** or **main processor**, is the component that processes or manipulates data. A processor can do nothing without a program to provide control; whatever intelligence a computer has is derived from software, not hardware. The processor manipulates data stored in its memory under the control of a program stored in its memory.

Instructions

A program consists of a series of **instructions**. Each instruction is a group of bits that tells the computer to perform one of its basic functions: add, subtract, multiply, divide, compare, copy, start input, or start output. Each instruction consists of two parts: an **operation code** and one or more **operands** (Fig. 2.8). The operation code tells the computer what to do (for example, add, subtract, or compare). The operands identify the memory locations or registers that hold the data to be manipulated by the instruction. For example, the instruction in Fig. 2.8 tells the computer to add the contents of memory locations 1000 and 1002.

program – instruction – (bits) operation code / operands

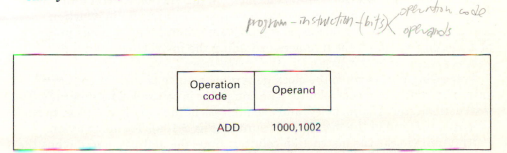

Operation code	Operand
ADD	1000,1002

Figure 2.8 An instruction is composed of an operation code and one or more operands. The operation code tells the computer what to do. The operand or operands identify the addresses of the data elements to be manipulated.

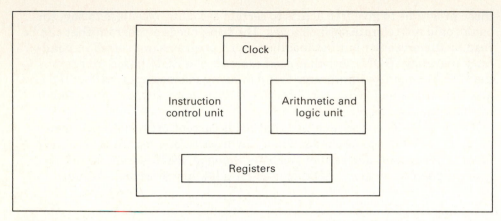

Figure 2.9 A processor contains four key components.

Processor Components

The processor contains four key components (Fig. 2.9): a clock, an instruction control unit, an arithmetic and logic unit, and a set of registers. The **clock** generates precisely timed pulses of current that synchronize the processor's other components. The **instruction control unit** determines the location of the next instruction to be executed and **fetches** it from memory. The **arithmetic and logic unit** executes that instruction; it consists of the circuits that add, subtract, multiply, divide, compare, copy, and initiate input or output—the computer's **instruction set**. **Registers** are temporary storage devices that hold control information, key data, and intermediate results.

Machine Cycles

Perhaps the best way to understand how a computer's internal components work is to observe a few **machine cycles**. Figure 2.10 is a simplified model of a computer. The processor contains a clock, an instruction control unit, an arithmetic and logic unit, and several registers, including an instruction counter, an instruction register, and an accumulator. Memory holds program instructions and data; the numbers preceding the instructions and data values are memory addresses.

Processing begins when the clock generates a pulse of current that activates the instruction control unit. The computer is controlled by program instructions stored in memory, and the address of the next instruction to be executed is found in the instruction counter (Fig. 2.10a). The instruction control unit checks the instruction counter, finds the address, and fetches the next instruction, placing it in the instruction register (Fig. 2.10b). Fetching an instruction from memory takes time, giving the instruction control unit an opportunity to increment the instruction counter to point to the next instruction; note in Fig. 2.10(b) that the instruction counter points to instruction 2.

The instruction control unit then activates the arithmetic and logic unit, which executes the instruction stored in the instruction register (Fig. 2.10c).

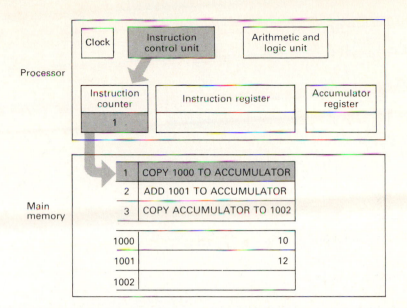

Figure 2.10 A computer executes one instruction during each machine cycle. **(a)** As the example begins, memory holds both program instructions and data. The instruction register points to the first instruction to be executed.

Thus a data value is copied from memory to the accumulator register, and the first machine cycle ends.

Once again, the clock "ticks," initiating the next machine cycle. The instruction control unit finds the address of its next instruction in the instruc-

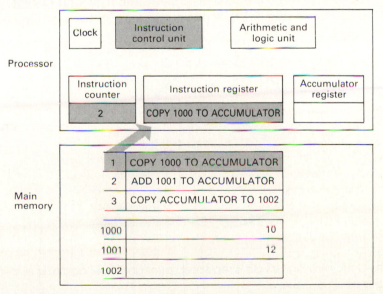

Figure 2.10(b) In response to a fetch command from the instruction control unit, the first instruction is copied from memory and stored in the instruction register. Note that the instruction counter points to the *next* instruction.

The Processor and Main Memory
The Processor

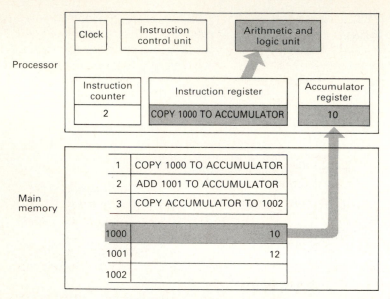

Figure 2.10(c) Next, the arithmetic and logic unit executes the instruction in the instruction register, ending the first machine cycle.

tion counter and fetches it from memory. Once the new instruction is in the instruction register, the arithmetic and logic unit executes it. This basic machine cycle continues until all the program's instructions have been executed.

An instruction is fetched by the instruction control unit during **instruction time (I-time)** and executed by the arithmetic and logic unit during **execution time (E-time)** (Fig. 2.11). This process is repeated over and over

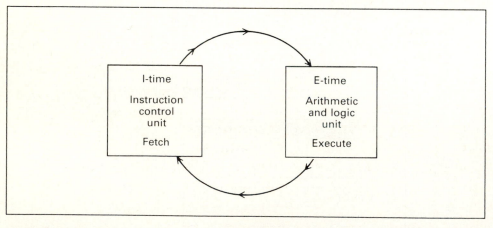

Figure 2.11 The basic machine cycle is repeated over and over again, until all the instructions have been executed.

again until the program is finished. The clock drives the process, generating pulses of current at precisely timed intervals. The rate at which the clock pulses are generated is what determines the computer's operating speed. On many modern computers, clock time is measured in nanoseconds (billionths of a second), so the machine can execute millions of instructions per second.

Summary

Internally, a computer is a binary machine, so data and program instructions must be stored in binary form. Characters are represented in a binary code. Numbers are stored as binary numbers, with each bit's positional value significant. A computer's main memory is divided into bytes, or words, or both (depending on the system), and each of these basic storage units is assigned a unique address. Using this address, the processor can read or write selected bytes or words.

The processor contains a clock, an instruction control unit, an arithmetic and logic unit, and registers. Once a program is stored in memory, the processor can begin to execute it. During I-time, the instruction control unit fetches an instruction from memory; during E-time, the arithmetic and logic unit executes it. Precisely timed electronic pulses generated by the clock drive this basic machine cycle, which is repeated over and over again until the program is completed.

Key Words

address

arithmetic and logic unit

binary

bit

byte

central processing unit (CPU)

clock

execution time (E-time)

fetch

instruction

instruction control unit

instruction set

instruction time (I-time)

machine cycle

main memory

main processor

operand

operation code

processor

random access memory (RAM)

register

read-only memory (ROM)

word

Self-Test

1. Positional values in the binary number system are factors of ___2___.
2. A physical switch is _hardware_; its setting is _software_.
3. A _byte_ holds enough bits to store a single character. A _word_ is a group of bytes large enough to hold a significant number.
4. Inside a computer, characters are represented by a binary _code_.
5. The "digit-times-place-value" rule works with _numbers_ but not with _characters_.
6. A location in memory is accessed by its _address_.
7. When memory is _read_, its contents are not changed. When memory is _write_, its contents are changed.
8. A programmer can read and write _RAM_, but _ROM_ can only be read.
9. The processor fetches and executes _instructions_.
10. The part of an instruction that tells the processor what to do is the _operation code_. The part of an instruction that identifies the memory locations or registers that hold the data to be manipulated by the instruction is (or are) the _operands_.
11. The processor's components are synchronized by _clock pulses_.
12. The processor's _instruction control unit_ fetches the next instruction from memory. The processor's _arithmetic and logic unit_ executes instructions.
13. Within the processor the _registers_ hold key control information such as the address of the next instruction to be executed.
14. An instruction is fetched during _I-time_ and executed during _E-time_.
15. One instruction is fetched and executed during a single _machine cycle_.

Relating the Concepts

1. Inside a computer, data are stored and manipulated in binary form. Why binary?
2. Distinguish between bits, bytes, and words.
3. How is a computer's main memory addressed?
4. Distinguish between a memory location's address and its contents.
5. Distinguish between ROM and RAM.
6. What is an instruction?
7. What happens during a single machine cycle? Relate the machine cycle to the computer's internal components; in other words, explain how those components work together to execute instructions.
8. What are registers? How are registers used?
9. In Chapter 1 (Exercise 7) you sketched the components of a typical computer system. In this chapter you studied the processor and memory in more detail. Add that detail to your sketch.

Input and Output

3

Preview

People communicate with a computer through its input and output devices. This chapter describes a number of common I/O devices and explains how they work. Key concepts include:

Accessing a computer

Basic I/O

- Keyboards and display screens
- Printers

Graphics

- Graphic output
- Graphic input

Other input and output devices

- Punched cards
- Printers
- Magnetic media

- Optical media
- Terminals
- Voice recognition/voice response

Accessing a Computer

A computer is a machine that processes data into information. Unless some human being needs the information, there is no point in processing the data. Input and output (I/O) devices provide a means for people to access a computer. This chapter describes a number of input and output devices and media.

Basic I/O

Keyboards and Display Screens

The basic input device on most small computer systems is a **keyboard** (Fig. 3.1). As characters are typed, they are stored in memory (Fig. 3.2a). From memory they are copied to the basic output device, a **display screen** (Fig. 3.2b). In effect, the screen (Fig. 3.3), sometimes called a monitor, serves as a window on memory, allowing the user to view selected contents.

Several different types of displays are available. Some show white characters against a black background; options include green and amber screens. Color monitors display characters, charts, pictures, and diagrams in color. Standard television sets are sometimes used as inexpensive display devices, but because the clarity of a television signal suffers when small elements (such as letters and digits) are displayed, real computer monitors produce a much sharper image.

Figure 3.1 The basic input device on most small computer systems is a keyboard. Courtesy of International Business Machines Corporation.

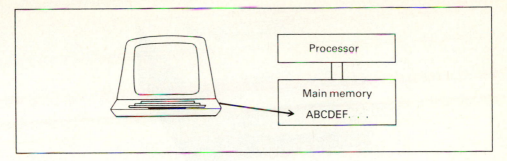

Figure 3.2(a) As characters are typed, they are stored in the computer's memory.

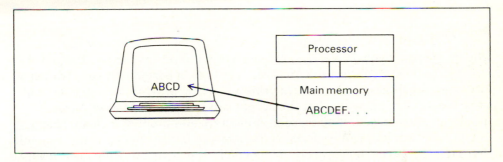

Figure 3.2(b) Selected characters are then output from memory to the display screen.

Figure 3.3 The basic output device on most small computer systems is a display screen. Courtesy of International Business Machines Corporation.

Figure 3.4 A printer generates more permanent hard-copy output. Courtesy of Hewlett-Packard Company.

Printers

The image displayed on a screen is temporary; it fades as soon as the power is cut. By routing the output to a **printer** (Fig. 3.4), a permanent copy (called a hard copy) is obtained. Dot matrix printers form characters from patterns of dots; they are inexpensive, but the output can be difficult to read. Letter-quality printers type complete, solid characters and produce a clean, sharp impression. Ink jet printers form characters and images by "spitting" tiny ink dots onto the paper. Laser printers are more expensive, but they print a very sharp image and can mix high-quality text and graphics on the same page.

Graphics

Graphic Output

Computers are not limited to displaying characters; **graphic** output (Fig. 3.5) is possible, too. Because a computer's output comes from memory, if a graphic image is to be displayed, it must first be constructed in memory. Memory stores bits. How can a cartoon character, a bar chart, or a schematic drawing be defined as a pattern of bits?

The secret is to divide the screen into a grid of picture elements, or **pixels** (Fig. 3.6). Each pixel represents a dot or a point; by selectively turning the points on or off, a picture is formed. The on/off state of each pixel is binary and can be stored in memory. As memory is scanned, the picture elements are displayed, and the image appears.

The quality, or **resolution**, of the picture is a function of the number of pixels. For example, a single, large picture element can show no detail; the screen is either all black or all white. With nine pixels (a 3 x 3 grid), it is possible to form a single, rough character, much as light bulbs form characters on a scoreboard. As the number of picture elements increases, finer and

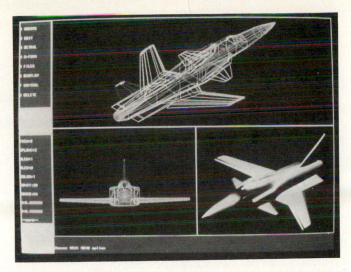

Figure 3.5 Increasingly, computers are being used to generate graphic output as well as character output. Courtesy of CADKEY, INC.

finer details can be displayed. Of course, there is a cost for this improvement; since information about each pixel must be stored, high-resolution graphics requires more memory than low-resolution graphics.

Graphic output displayed on a screen is temporary. For a hard copy, the image can be sent to a plotter (Fig. 3.7). Some dot matrix printers and most ink jet and laser printers can also output graphic images.

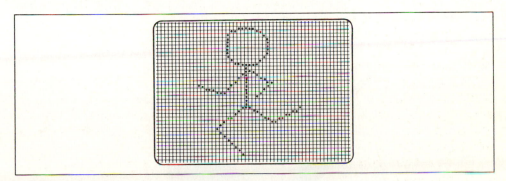

Figure 3.6 To display graphic output, the screen is divided into a grid of picture elements, or pixels. Each pixel represents one point. Pictures are formed by turning selected pixels on and off.

Input and Output Graphics

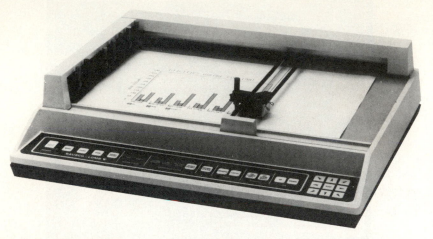

Figure 3.7 A plotter generates permanent hard-copy graphic output. Courtesy of Houston Instrument Division AMETEK, Inc.

Graphic Input

How might a person manipulate or interact with a picture once it is displayed? One way to generate graphic input is by controlling the cursor. Usually seen as a blinking line or a box, the **cursor** indicates the position where the next character typed will appear. By moving the cursor to point to a menu choice or an icon, the user communicates a command or a desired action to the computer.

Perhaps the best-known device for controlling the cursor is a joystick (Fig. 3.8); if you have ever played a computer game, you have probably used one. Similar cursor control can be obtained with a mouse (Fig. 3.9), a small, palm-

Figure 3.8 Perhaps the best-known device for controlling the cursor is the joystick. Courtesy of Apple Computer, Inc.

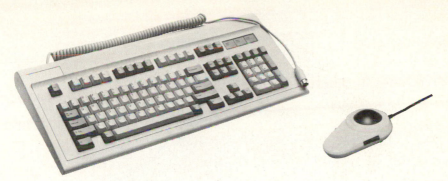

Figure 3.9 The cursor's position can also be changed by manipulating a mouse or by pressing the keyboard's cursor control keys. Courtesy of Cortron, a Division of Illinois Tool Works, Inc.

sized device with a roller on the bottom. The mouse is placed on a flat surface. Move it forward, and the cursor moves up; move it to the left, and the cursor moves to the left, and so on. Like a joystick, a mouse moves the cursor relative to its present position. The cursor control keys found on many keyboards perform the same function.

The cursor's position defines a point on the screen. Pushing a button on a joystick or a mouse or pressing the enter key inputs the cursor's current position. Given the cursor's position, the stored program can take appropriate action. With a touch screen (Fig. 3.10), a user enters a point by touching a spot on the screen.

Figure 3.10 A touch screen can be used to input the *x-y* coordinates of selected points. Courtesy of Hewlett-Packard Company.

**Input and Output
Graphics**

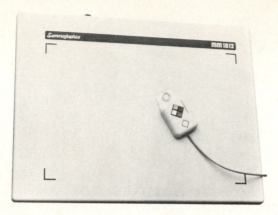

Figure 3.11 Graphic data can be input to a computer with a digitizer. Key points are entered relative to a fixed reference. Later, a plotter can reproduce the drawing by connecting the points. Courtesy of Summagraphics Corporation.

A digitizer (Fig. 3.11) is used to input graphic data. The source document (an engineering drawing, for example) is placed on a tablet, and a reference (often the lower left corner or the center) is established. Next, the digitizer is

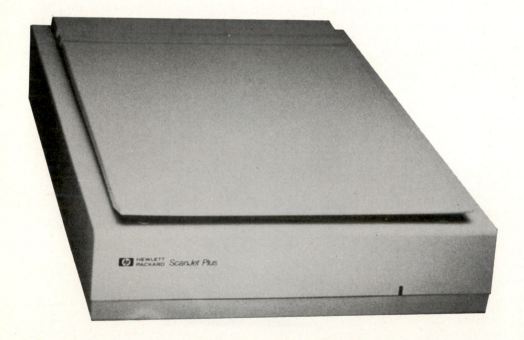

Figure 3.12 Graphic images can also be captured by a scanner. Courtesy of Hewlett-Packard.

moved to a significant point such as the juncture of two lines, a button is pushed, and the point's x-y coordinates are transmitted into the computer. The user enters all the key points by moving the digitizer methodically over the source document. Later, a plotter can reproduce the drawing by connecting the points.

Graphic images can also be captured by a scanner (Fig. 3.12). Most scanners work much like an office copier. Basically, the image is converted to a grid of black dots and the dot/no-dot pattern is stored as a set of bits or pixels. Later, the bit pattern can be used to reproduce the image.

Other Input and Output Devices

Punched Cards

Punched cards were among the very first computer input media. A standard card is composed of 80 columns, each divided into 12 rows. As characters are typed through a keypunch, they are recorded as patterns of holes in a column; for each possible row/column position there either is or is not a hole. A card reader converts the hole patterns to electronic form. Note that the card's hole/no hole pattern is essentially binary.

Printers

Most microcomputer printers output one character at a time, usually at rates varying from 30 to perhaps 180 characters per second. Their speed is fine for producing a few pages, but imagine printing a 200-page accounting report at 100 characters per second. Assuming a 120-character line and 50 lines per page, the report would take over three hours to print!

A more reasonable approach is to use a line printer (Fig. 3.13), which, as the name implies, prints line by line instead of character by character. Rates of 1000 lines per minute (and more) are common; at 1000 lines per minute the accounting report described above could be printed in ten minutes. Even greater speed can be obtained by using a page printer to churn out complete pages at a time. For more compact output or long-term storage, computer output microfilm (COM) can be used.

Magnetic Media

Several common input media rely on **magnetic** properties. For example, the characters on the bottom of a check (Fig. 3.14) are printed with a special magnetic ink called MICR (magnetic ink character recognition) and can be read electronically. Magnetic strip cards (Fig. 3.15) are another banking medium. The strip of magnetic tape holds such data as a customer's account number and credit limit and is read much like sound recording tape.

Figure 3.13 A line printer prints a complete line at one time. Courtesy of Dataproducts Corporation.

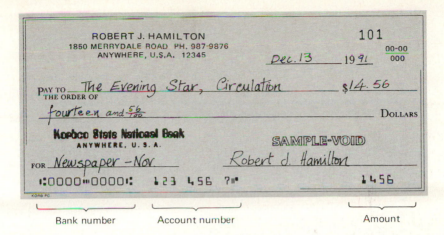

Figure 3.14 Most bank checks are printed using a magnetic ink called MICR.

Optical Media

Other media are read **optically**. For example, consider standardized test forms (Fig. 3.16). Students use a black pencil to mark their answers. The white paper reflects light; the black spots reflect much less; variations in the intensity of the reflected light can be converted to an electronic pattern. OCR (optical character recognition) equipment uses the same principle to read typed or even handwritten material. Bar codes, such as the Universal Product Code (UPC) printed on most supermarket packages, can be read at a checkout station (Fig. 3.17) or by a hand-held scanner (Fig. 3.18).

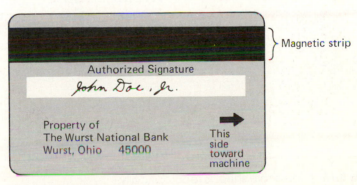

Figure 3.15 A magnetic strip card.

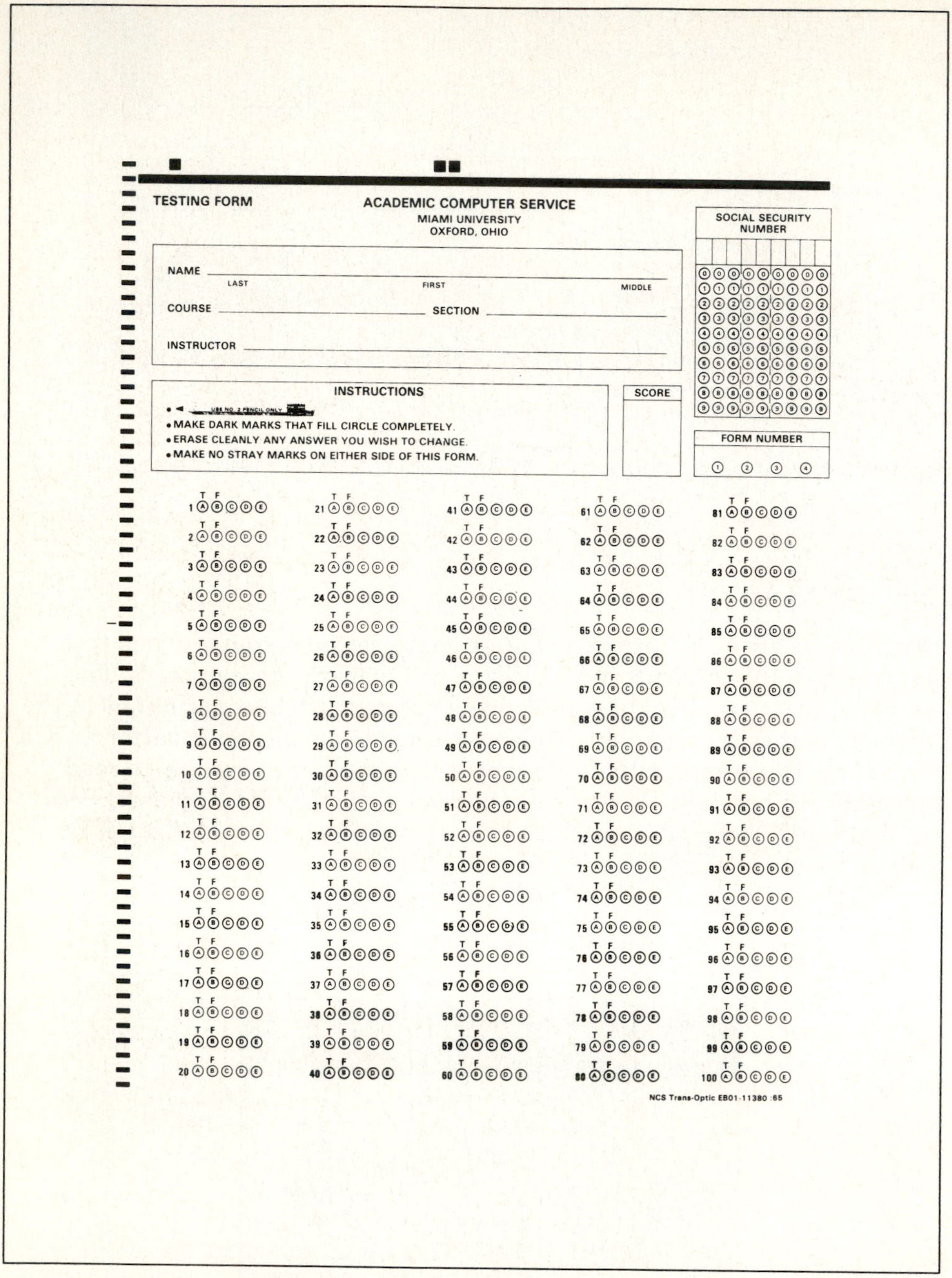
TESTING FORM

ACADEMIC COMPUTER SERVICE
MIAMI UNIVERSITY
OXFORD, OHIO

SOCIAL SECURITY NUMBER

NAME
LAST FIRST MIDDLE

COURSE SECTION

INSTRUCTOR

INSTRUCTIONS
• USE NO. 2 PENCIL ONLY
• MAKE DARK MARKS THAT FILL CIRCLE COMPLETELY.
• ERASE CLEANLY ANY ANSWER YOU WISH TO CHANGE.
• MAKE NO STRAY MARKS ON EITHER SIDE OF THIS FORM.

SCORE

FORM NUMBER

NCS Trans-Optic EB01-11380 :65

Figure 3.16 A test score sheet is read optically.

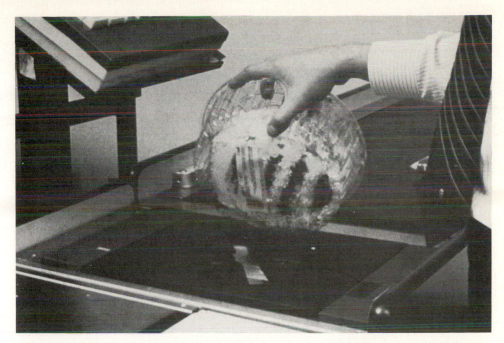

Figure 3.17 Supermarket checkout stations contain built-in scanners to read the universal product code printed on most packages. Courtesy of ICL Retail Systems, Dallas, Texas.

Figure 3.18 Hand-held scanners can also read the universal product code. They are often used by sales personnel to collect inventory and sales data. Courtesy of ICL Retail Systems, Dallas, Texas.

Figure 3.19 A terminal is a keyboard/display unit linked to a central computer via some type of communication line.

Terminals

Terminals (Fig. 3.19) are also popular. Often, a hundred or more terminals are linked to a central computer by communication lines. A "dumb" terminal is simply a keyboard and a display screen. An intelligent terminal contains its own memory and processor and can perform many data processing functions on its own. Other, special-purpose terminals are designed for a specific function. Examples include automatic bank teller terminals and the supermarket checkout station described previously.

Voice Recognition/Voice Response

Perhaps the most natural way of communicating with a computer is by **voice**. Voice response (output) is already used in such mundane applications as children's toys and video games. Due to the tremendous variety of human speech patterns, voice recognition (input) is much more difficult, but significant advances have been made. For certain limited applications, voice recognition is already here (Fig. 3.20).

Figure 3.20 For certain limited applications, voice recognition equipment is already available. Courtesy of MLS/A-Dan Murray.

Summary

People access a computer through its input and output devices. The basic input device on most small computers is the keyboard. As a user types characters, they are stored in memory; from there, they are output to a display screen. If a permanent copy of the output is required, it can be sent to a printer.

Many systems support graphics. A screen is divided into a number of points called pixels, and images are formed by selectively turning the pixels on and off. Hard-copy graphic output is generated by a plotter. Graphic images can be input by using a digitizer or a scanner. There are many other input and output devices and media, including punched cards, various types of printers, magnetic media, optical media, terminals, and voice I/O.

Key Words

cursor

display screen

graphics

keyboard

magnetic media

optical media

pixel

printer

punched card

resolution

terminal

voice I/O

Self-Test

1. The basic input device on a small computer is a _keyboard_.
2. The basic output device on a small computer is a _display screen_
3. A _printer_ generates hard-copy output.
4. A display screen is divided into a grid of _pixels_.
5. The _cursor_ indicates where on the screen the next character will appear.
6. Graphic images can be input to a computer by using a _scanner_ or a _digitizer_.
7. On a _punched card_, data are recorded as patterns of holes.
8. The characters on the bottom of a check are read _magnetically_.
9. Standardized test forms are read _optically_.
10. Often, a hundred or more _terminals_ are linked to a centralized computer by communication lines.

Relating the Concepts

1. What is the function of a computer's input and output devices?
2. List several input devices. List several output devices. How can you tell which is which? Don't just cite the book. Think about your answer.
3. Briefly distinguish between dot matrix, letter quality, ink jet, and laser printers.
4. What is a pixel? Relate pixels to a screen's resolution.
5. What is a cursor? List several devices for controlling the cursor's position.
6. Briefly explain how graphic data can be input to a computer.
7. Why are high-speed line and page printers necessary?
8. Briefly explain how magnetic media work.
9. Briefly explain how optical media work.
10. Although effective voice recognition/voice response I/O is not yet widely available, many experts expect such equipment to have a significant impact in the future. Why?

4

Secondary Storage

Preview

Secondary storage devices, such as magnetic disk, support the long-term storage of large amounts of data. This chapter describes a number of secondary storage devices and explains how they work. Key concepts include:

Why secondary storage?

Secondary storage media

- Diskette
- Hard disk
- Other secondary storage media

Accessing secondary storage

- The directory
- Secondary storage and main memory

Why Secondary Storage?

One advantage of a computer is that once data have been entered, they can be stored on the machine and accessed repeatedly. For example, a magazine publisher generates a set of address labels for each issue. Instead of retyping all the labels, subscriber data are input once, stored, and then dumped from storage whenever necessary. Programs provide another example. The instructions are not retyped each time the program is used. Instead, like the subscriber data, they are stored on the computer and accessed on demand.

Where exactly are the data and the programs stored? The obvious answer is in memory, but main memory is expensive, and the supply on most machines is limited. Volatility is another problem; main memory loses its contents when the power is cut. What is needed is a fast, accurate, inexpensive, high-capacity nonvolatile extension of main memory. **Secondary storage** fills this need.

Secondary Storage Media

Diskette

The most common microcomputer secondary storage medium is **diskette** (Fig. 4.1), a thin circular piece of polyester coated with a magnetic material. Data are recorded on one or both surfaces. Because contact with dust, lint, or even a human finger can destroy the data, each diskette has its own protective jacket. Until recently, flexible 5 1/4-inch **floppy disks** were the accepted standard, but many newer microcomputers use rigid, higher-capacity 3 1/2-inch **disks**. A typical 5 1/4-inch diskette can store 360KB (kilobytes) of data; 3 1/2-inch disks can store 720KB or even 1.44 MB (megabytes).

A diskette drive works much like a record turntable. The hole in the center of a floppy disk allows the drive mechanism to engage and spin it; an **access mechanism**, analogous to the tone arm, reads and writes the surface through a window near the bottom of the jacket. The drive hole is on the back of a 3 1/2-inch disk; the metal shield near the top moves aside to reveal the recording surface when the disk is inserted into the drive.

Figure 4.1 The most popular microcomputer secondary storage medium is diskette.

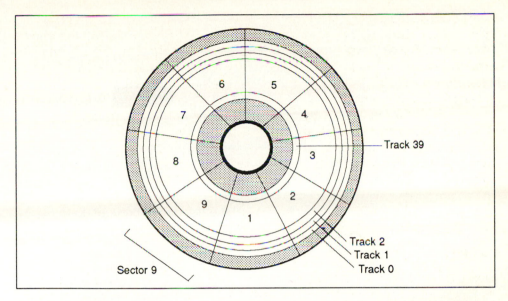

Figure 4.2 Data are recorded on a series of concentric circles called tracks. The tracks are subdivided into sectors. Data move between the disk surface and memory one sector at a time.

Data are recorded on a series of concentric circles called **tracks** (Fig. 4.2). The access mechanism steps from track to track, reading or writing one at a time. The tracks are subdivided into **sectors**; it is the contents of a sector that move between the diskette and memory. To distinguish the sectors, they are addressed by numbering them sequentially.

When a program instruction requesting diskette input is encountered, the processor sends a control signal to the drive. In response, the drive spindle is engaged and the disk begins to spin, quickly reaching a constant rotational speed (Fig. 4.3a). Next, the access mechanism is moved to the track containing the desired data (Fig. 4.3b). The time required to bring the drive up to speed and position the access mechanism is called **seek time**. Remember that data are transferred between the diskette and memory a sector at a time. The desired sector may be anywhere on the track. The time required for the sector to rotate to the access mechanism (Fig. 4.3c) is called **rotational delay**.

Accessing the data stored on a diskette means a delay of at least a fraction of a second. Many common personal computer applications involve only limited disk access, so the delay is hardly noticeable, but on other applications it can be intolerable. The solution is a hard disk.

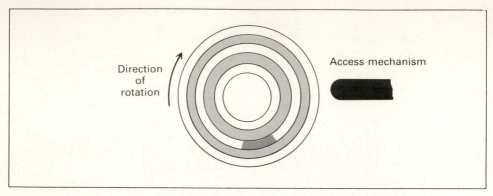

Figure 4.3 Reading a sector from disk. **(a)** First the disk drive is brought up to operating speed.

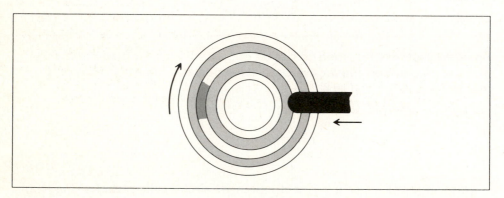

Figure 4.3(b) Next, the access mechanism is positioned over the track that holds the desired data. The time required to perform steps a and b is called seek time.

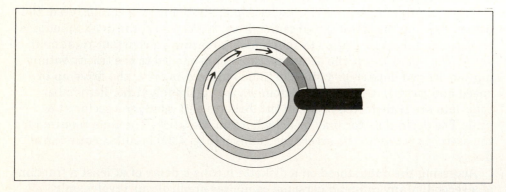

Figure 4.3(c) Finally, the system waits until the desired sector rotates to the read/write head (rotational delay) before the data are transferred into memory.

Hard Disk

A diskette drive spins only when data are being read or written. The drive must be brought up to operating speed before the read/write heads can be moved and the data accessed, and that takes time. A **hard disk** (Fig. 4.4), in contrast, spins constantly. Since it is not necessary to wait for the drive to reach operating speed before moving the access mechanism, seek time is significantly reduced, often to a few thousandths of a second. Further improvements are gained by spinning the disk more rapidly (1000 revolutions per minute or more), which reduces rotational delay. Data on hard disk can be accessed far more quickly than data on diskette.

Another advantage of hard disk is its storage capacity. For example, a high-density 3 1/2-inch diskette can hold 1.44MB of data, and a hard disk, even on a microcomputer, can store 20MB, 40MB, or even more data.

With slow diskette drives, the access mechanism rides directly on the disk surface. At 1000 revolutions per minute, however, any physical contact between the disk surface and the read/write head would quickly destroy both, so a hard disk's access mechanism rides on a cushion of air, a few millionths of an inch above the surface (Fig. 4.5). (Shaped like an airfoil, the access mechanism literally flies.) Such pollutants as a smoke particle, dust, or a human hair could cause serious damage because they won't fit between the head and the surface, so a hard disk is normally encased in an airtight container to protect it from the environment.

Figure 4.4 Hard disk is faster than diskette and has a greater storage capacity. Photo courtesy of Seagate Technology.

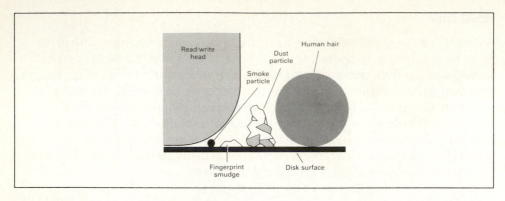

Figure 4.5 A hard disk's access mechanism rides on a cushion of air a few millionths of an inch above the disk surface.

Although single-surface disks do exist, particularly on small systems, most large computers use **disk packs** consisting of several recording surfaces stacked on a common drive shaft (Fig. 4.6). Typically, each surface has its own read/write head. The heads are arrayed on a single, comblike access mechanism, and they all move together. Imagine, for example, that the access mechanism is positioned over track 30. The top read/write head will access track 30 on surface 0. Moving down, surface by surface, the second head will be over track 30 on surface 1, the third over track 30 on surface 2, and so on.

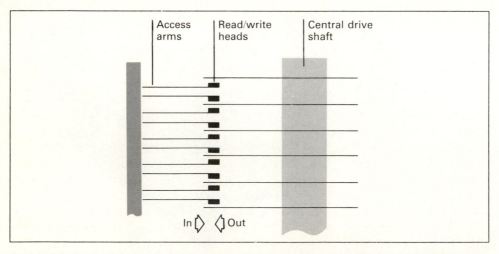

Figure 4.6 On a disk pack, each surface has its own read/write head. The heads are arrayed on a single, comb-like access mechanism, so they all move together.

Figure 4.7 A typical disk pack. Courtesy of NCR Corporation.

One position of the access mechanism corresponds to one track on each surface. This set of tracks is called a **cylinder**.

Accessing disk begins with seek time. The access mechanism is moved to a selected cylinder, and a selected head is activated. The system is now looking at a single track. Next, the desired data rotate to the read/write head (rotational delay). Finally, the data are transferred into the computer.

A disk pack, such as the one shown in Fig. 4.7, is mounted on a disk drive containing a spindle and an access mechanism. Some packs are fixed; others can be changed. If a disk pack is dismounted, a different pack's data can be accessed through the same set of read/write heads. With Winchester technology the pack and the access mechanism are sealed together in an airtight container, giving each pack its own set of heads. Winchester disks are popular on smaller computer systems.

A disk pack contains several recording surfaces, so packs that can hold hundreds of megabytes of data are common. Most large computers support numerous disk packs. Consequently, it is not unusual for a single computer to have gigabytes (billions of bytes) of secondary storage capacity.

Given the tremendous capacity of a disk pack, losing one through human error, fire, flood, or similar disaster can destroy a great deal of important data. In most large computer centers the data are regularly backed up by copying them to another medium. Should a disk pack be lost, the **backup** copy is used to restore the data.

Figure 4.8 Magnetic tape is a common backup medium. Courtesy of Kennedy Company, Monrovia, California.

Other Secondary Storage Media

Magnetic tape (Fig. 4.8) is a popular backup medium. Tape is fast, with data transfer rates comparable to disk. Its storage capacity is quite high, and a reel of tape is relatively inexpensive. Unfortunately, data can be read or written only in a fixed order, which limits tape to sequential applications.

The original secondary storage device was **magnetic drum**. As the name implies, a drum is a cylinder coated on the outside surface with the same magnetic material that coats disk and tape. Data are stored on parallel tracks that encircle the surface. Each track has its own read/write head. Since no head movement is required, there is no seek time; magnetic drum is very fast. However, in comparison to disk, drum has limited storage capacity and is quite expensive.

Video disk is one of the newer secondary storage media. These disks are read and written by a laser beam, so there is no physical contact between the recording surface and the read/write mechanism. Fast, accurate, compact, and easy to use, video disk has a promising future.

CD-ROM (compact disk read-only memory) is another promising medium. It provides tremendous storage capacity at a relatively low cost. Already, numerous references such as dictionaries, encyclopedias, and technical manuals are available on CD-ROM, and this medium's ability to store sophisticated graphic images suggests a number of exciting near-future applications.

Accessing Secondary Storage

The Directory

Because of its storage capacity, a single disk can hold hundreds of programs or the data for dozens of different applications. If you are a computer user, however, you want a particular program, and you want to access a particular set of data. How does the computer find the right program or the right data?

Start by reviewing how data are stored on disk. The surface is divided into tracks, which in turn are divided into sectors. Data are stored in the sectors as patterns of bits. The tracks are numbered sequentially. The outer track is 0. Moving toward the center of the disk, the next track is 1, then 2, and so on. The sectors are also numbered sequentially. The first sector on a track is 1, the second is 2, then 3, and so on. Track 5, sector 8 is a particular sector; track 5, sector 9 is a different sector; and track 6, sector 8 is yet another one. Each sector on the disk has a unique track/sector address.

When a program is stored on disk, it is normally recorded in a set of consecutive sectors. If the program starts on track 3, sector 1, you can assume that it is continued on track 3, sector 2, and so on. If the computer can find a program's first sector, it can find the entire program.

To help the system determine where a particular program begins on disk, several sectors on the first track are set aside to hold an index or **directory** (Fig. 4.9). When the program is first written to disk, it is assigned a name,

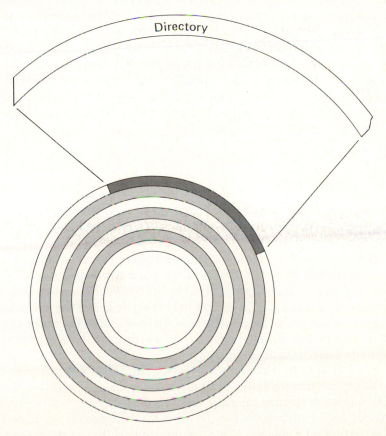

Figure 4.9 A directory is maintained to keep track of the programs and data files stored on disk.

and that name, along with the track and sector address where the program begins, is recorded in the directory. Later, to retrieve the program, a user enters the program's name. The computer then reads the directory, searches it for the name, finds the address where the program begins, and reads the program.

Data are accessed in much the same way. The data for a given application are grouped to form a file; data files will be covered in Chapter 8. Each file is assigned a name. The file name and the address of its first sector are recorded in the disk's directory. Because the data that make up a file are normally stored in consecutive sectors, knowing the first sector's address allows the system to find the others.

Secondary Storage and Main Memory

Secondary storage is an extension of main memory, not a replacement for it. A computer cannot execute a program stored on disk unless the program is first copied into memory. A computer cannot manipulate the data stored on a secondary medium until the data have been copied into memory. Main memory holds the current program and the current data; secondary storage is long-term storage.

The input and output devices described in Chapter 3 provide human access to the computer system. Secondary storage does not. Data are stored on disk in a form that is convenient to the computer and can be read and written only by the machine. The only way people can access the data stored on a disk is by instructing the computer to read them into main memory and then output them to a display screen or a printer.

Summary

Because of its cost, limited capacity, and volatility, main memory cannot be used for long-term or for volume storage. Secondary storage is a solution.

Magnetic diskette is the most popular secondary storage medium. Data are stored on a series of concentric circles called tracks, which are subdivided into sectors. It is the contents of a sector that move between memory and the disk's surface. To access disk, it is first necessary to bring the drive up to operating speed and then move the access mechanism to the track containing the data (seek time). Additional time is lost waiting for the sector to rotate to the read/write head (rotational delay).

Unlike diskette, hard disk spins constantly, and that reduces seek time. Because hard disk rotates faster than diskette, it has less rotational delay. Hard disk has more storage capacity, too. On diskette the read/write head rides directly on the disk surface; with hard disk the access mechanism rides above the surface on a cushion of air. Often, several disks are stacked on a single drive shaft to form a disk pack. A disk pack normally has one read/write head per surface. The heads are grouped on a single access mechanism; one position of the access mechanism defines a cylinder.

Because data are so valuable, disk packs are normally backed up. Magnetic tape is a common backup medium. The first secondary storage medium was magnetic drum. Video disk and CD-ROM show promise for the future.

A single disk can contain numerous programs and data files. The disk's directory identifies the programs and files and indicates the track and sector address where each one begins. Given the address of the first sector, the other sectors can be located.

Secondary storage is an extension of main memory. The computer cannot execute a program until it has been loaded into memory, nor can it process data until they have been copied into memory. Secondary storage cannot be read by human beings; it is a machine-readable medium.

Key Words

access mechanism	hard disk
backup	magnetic drum
CD-ROM	magnetic tape
cylinder	rotational delay
directory	secondary storage
disk	sector
diskette	seek time
disk pack	track
floppy disk	video disk

Self-Test

1. Main memory is _volatile_; it loses its contents when power is cut.
2. The most common microcomputer secondary storage medium is _diskette_.
3. Data on disk are recorded on a series of concentric circles called _track_.
4. Data are transferred between main memory and the disk surface a _sector_ at a time.
5. The time delay during which the disk drive is brought up to operating speed and the access mechanism is positioned is called _seek time_.
6. The time during which the desired sector rotates to the access mechanism is called _rotational time_.
7. A _hard disk_ rotates constantly.
8. Hard disk rotates faster than diskette, and that reduces _rotational time_.
9. Several disks stacked on a single drive spindle form a _disk pack_.

10. On a disk pack, one position of the access mechanism accesses a set of tracks called a ___cylinder___.

11. ___Magnetic tape___ is a popular backup medium.

12. Two secondary storage media that show promise for the near future are ___CD ROM___ and ___video disk___.

13. The combination of a sector number and a track number forms a unique disk ___address___.

14. The address of the beginning of each program stored on a disk is found in the disk's ___directory___.

15. ___Secondary storage___ is an extension to main memory, not a replacement for it.

Relating the Concepts

1. Why is secondary storage necessary?

2. Imagine a set of data stored in main memory. Explain the process of transferring the data to disk. Be specific; explain each step in the process.

3. What is the difference between a diskette and a hard disk? What advantages are gained by using hard disk?

4. What is a disk pack?

5. Distinguish between a cylinder, a track, and a sector.

6. What is backup? Why is backup necessary?

7. Explain how a computer finds the "right" data or the "right" program stored on disk.

8. Secondary storage is an extension of main memory. Explain.

Linking the Components

5

Preview

This chapter explains how a computer's hardware components are physically linked to form a complete computer system. Key concepts include:

Micros, minis, and mainframes

- Bus lines and cables
- Word size

Microcomputer architecture

- Motherboards and slots
- Interfaces
- Loading and executing a program

Mainframe architecture

- Concurrent processing
- Channels and control units
- Multiple bus lines

Micros, Minis, and Mainframes

To this point, you have studied a computer's primary components one by one. You know that a computer contains a processor and memory and that numerous input, output, and secondary storage devices can be attached, but you probably tend to view those components as independent boxes. It's time to link the pieces. In this chapter, you'll investigate how a computer's components are assembled.

Bus Lines and Cables

Data, instructions, and control signals flow between components in response to instructions executed by the processor. Some components are linked by **parallel** lines that consist of several wires. In contrast, a **serial** line is a single wire. Clearly, in a given amount of time, more cars can cross a four-lane bridge than can cross a one-lane bridge, and the same logic holds for serial and parallel lines. Because they can move several bits at the same time, parallel lines are faster.

Bus lines, such as the ribbonlike set of wires pictured in Fig. 5.1, link the computer's internal components and are used to attach secondary storage devices to the system. They transmit data in parallel. Input and output devices are connected to the system by **cables**. Parallel cables contain several wires and are used to link fast peripherals. Serial cables consist of a single wire and are used with slower peripherals.

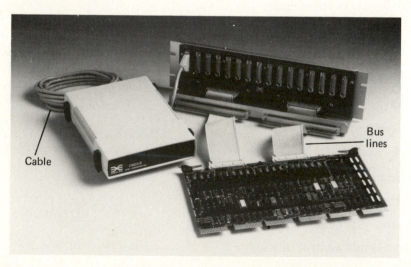

Cable

Bus lines

Figure 5.1 A computer's internal components are linked by ribbon-like bus lines. External devices are attached to the system by cables.

Word Size

Communication between the components is greatly simplified if they are electronically similar. On most systems the processor, main memory, busses, interfaces, and channels are all designed around a common **word** size. For example, on a 32-bit computer the processor manipulates 32-bit numbers, main memory and the registers store 32-bit words, and data and instructions move between the components over 32-bit bus lines. Almost any word size can be used, although 4, 8, 16, and 32 bits are the most common.

A 32-bit bus contains 32 wires and thus can carry 32 bits at a time. A 16-bit bus has only 16 parallel wires and can carry only 16. Because the wider bus moves twice as much data in the same amount of time, the 32-bit machine is clearly faster. Generally, the bigger the word size, the faster the computer can transmit data between components.

Memory capacity is also a function of word size. To access memory, the processor must transmit over a bus the address of a desired instruction or data element. On a 32-bit machine a 32-bit address can be transmitted. The biggest 32-bit number is roughly 4 billion in decimal terms, so the processor can access as many as 4 billion different memory locations. On the other hand, a 16-bit computer transmits a 16-bit address, limiting it to roughly 64,000 memory locations. Generally, the bigger its word size, the more memory a computer can access.

There are 16-bit microcomputers that access considerably more than 64K bytes of memory. How is that possible? A 16-bit machine can access more than 64K if addresses are broken into two or more parts and transmitted during successive machine cycles. Each cycle takes time, however, so memory capacity is gained at the expense of processing speed.

Next, consider the size of the numbers each machine can manipulate. A 16-bit computer works with 16-bit numbers; a 32-bit machine works with 32-bit numbers. More digits mean more precise answers. Many 16-bit computers can transfer and work with 32-bit numbers but need two cycles to fetch the number from memory and two more to manipulate it. On a smaller machine, precision—like memory capacity—is achieved at the expense of processing speed.

Some inexpensive **microcomputers** are designed around an 8-bit word, and that limits their memory capacity, processing speed, and precision. More expensive micros and some **minicomputers** use a 16-bit word, giving them greater speed, more memory, and greater precision. Today, the trend is toward more powerful, faster, and more precise 32-bit micros and minis. Most **mainframes** are constructed around a 32-bit word. Some expensive scientific "supercomputers" have a 60- or 64-bit word.

Word size also influences a system's cost. Most 8-bit machines are priced well under $1000, while more powerful micros sell for $2000 or more. A basic minicomputer costs about $10,000, while a mainframe might sell for $100,000, and most supercomputers exceed $1 million. There is a great deal

Computer Type	Word Size	Cycle Time	Memory Capacity	Cost	Examples
Home micro	8–16 bits	microseconds	640KB	About $1000	Apple IIc, Apple IIe
Professional micro	16–32 bits	a microsecond	1 megabyte	Over $2000	IBM PC, IBM PS/2
Mini	16–32 bits	50 nanoseconds	10 megabytes	$10,000+	DEC PDP series
Mainframe	32 bits	25 nanoseconds	50 megabytes	$100,000+	IBM 3083, 4361
Super	64 bits	10 nanoseconds	50 megabytes	$1 million+	Cray X-MP/2

Figure 5.2 A comparison of computer types.

of overlap, with inexpensive 16-bit "minis" competing with surprisingly powerful 32-bit "supermicros," and "superminis" performing traditional mainframe tasks. The terms "micro," "mini," and "mainframe" are guidelines, not absolutes (Fig. 5.2).

Discussing such factors as word size, bus width, speed, memory capacity, precision, and cost makes it easy to overlook the obvious. Microcomputers (Fig. 5.3) are small and have a limited number of peripherals. Mainframes

Figure 5.3 A typical microcomputer system. Courtesy of International Business Machines Corporation.

Figure 5.4 A mainframe computer system. Courtesy of International Business Machines Corporation.

(Fig. 5.4), on the other hand, are much larger and typically support a vast array of input, output, and secondary storage devices. Generally, a microcomputer is used by a single person to perform a single task, a minicomputer is for multiple users who share a common application, and a mainframe supports multiple users performing multiple independent tasks.

Microcomputer Architecture

If you were to remove the cover from a microcomputer and a mainframe, you'd see that, although both contain similar components, they are assembled in different ways. Computer scientists use the term **architecture** when discussing the relationships between a system's components.

Motherboards and Slots

Most microcomputer systems are constructed around a **motherboard** (Fig. 5.5), a metal framework containing a series of **slots** linked, through a bus, to a 16- or 32-bit processor (Fig. 5.6). Memory is added by plugging a memory board into one of the open slots (Fig. 5.7). Without input and output the computer is useless, so a keyboard/display interface is plugged into another slot, and a keyboard and a display unit are attached (Fig. 5.8). A printer can be accessed through a printer interface, and, if a diskette interface is plugged into an open slot, a diskette drive can be added.

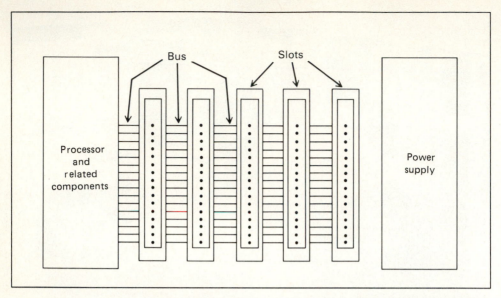

Figure 5.5 A microcomputer is constructed around a metal framework called a motherboard. Typically, the processor and related components are mounted on the motherboard, and a bus links the processor to a series of slots that are used to attach other boards to the system.

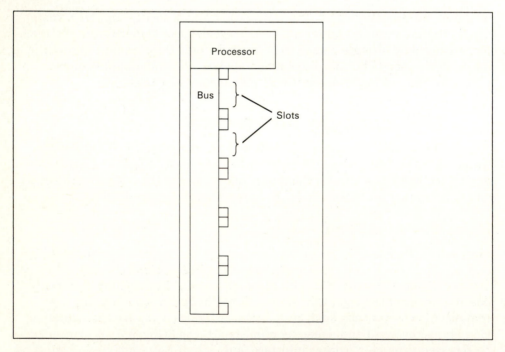

Figure 5.6 A schematic drawing showing a processor and a motherboard. A bus links the processor with a number of slots into which components can be plugged.

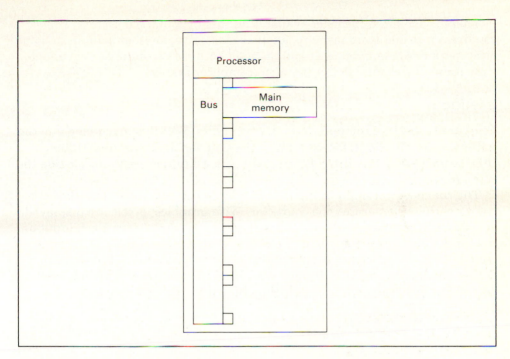

Figure 5.7 A memory board is plugged into one of the open slots.

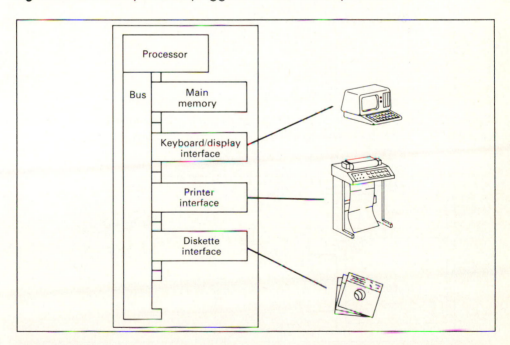

Figure 5.8 Input devices, output devices, and secondary storage devices are added to the system by plugging the appropriate interface into an open slot and then running a cable from the external device to the interface.

There is one more open slot available on this hypothetical system. You could use it to add more memory, another disk drive, another printer, or some other peripheral, but you can't add them all because the number of available slots limits the expandability of a microcomputer system.

Interfaces

Data are stored in a computer as patterns of bits. Within a given machine the patterns are consistent; for example, if the code for the letter A is 01000001, this pattern—and only this pattern—will be used to represent an A inside the computer.

The rule does not apply to input or output devices, however. On a keyboard, each key generates one character. With graphics, pixels are displayed. A dot matrix printer represents characters as patterns of dots. Each input or output device represents or interprets data in its own unique way, and the signals used by a peripheral device might or might not match the signals stored inside the computer. If these dissimilar devices are to communicate, translation is necessary. This is the function of the **interface** board.

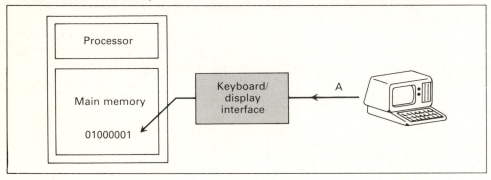

Figure 5.9 The functions of an interface board. **(a)** Input from the keyboard enters the interface and is converted to the computer's internal form.

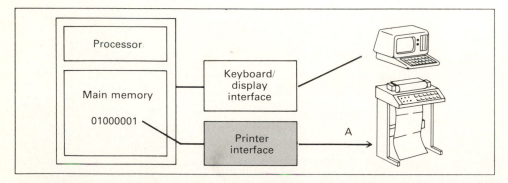

Figure 5.9(b) Data stored in main memory are sent to the printer interface, converted to printer form, and output.

Consider, for example, a keyboard. When a key is pressed, an electronic signal is sent to the keyboard's interface. In response, the interface generates the code used to represent that character inside the computer and transfers the coded data into memory (Fig. 5.9a). Change the device to a printer (Fig. 5.9b). As output begins, the data are stored inside the computer as binary-coded characters. The printer requires a dot pattern. Clearly, translation is necessary. The coded characters are sent to the printer's interface, which translates the computer's binary codes to printer form.

The printer and the keyboard are different; the signals that physically control them and the electronic patterns they use to represent data are device-dependent. However, because the device-dependent tasks are assigned to the respective interface boards, both can be attached to the same computer. On input, an interface board translates external signals into a form acceptable to the computer. Output signals are electronically converted from the computer's internal code to a form acceptable to the peripheral device. Because they are electronically different, a printer and a keyboard require different interface boards. In fact, every input or output device needs a unique interface board to translate its device-dependent signals to (or from) the computer's internal code.

Secondary storage devices are linked to a microcomputer through interface boards, too. The interface board physically controls the disk drive, accepting seek, read, and write commands from the processor, positioning the access mechanism, and controlling the flow of data between the disk surface and memory.

Loading and Executing a Program

The components that compose a typical microcomputer are linked by a common bus. This arrangement is called **single-bus architecture** (Fig. 5.10). All communications between components flow over this bus, under control of the processor.

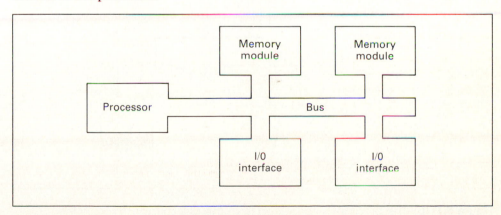

Figure 5.10 A typical microcomputer uses a single-bus architecture, with all internal components linked by a single bus line.

Consider the process of loading and executing a program on a single-bus computer. First, in response to a user's command, a control signal is sent over the bus to the disk interface (Fig. 5.11a). Responding to the signal, the interface causes the disk drive to read the program and transfer it, over the bus, into memory (Fig. 5.11b). Once the program is in memory, the processor can execute it, fetching its instructions, over the bus, one by one (Fig. 5.11c).

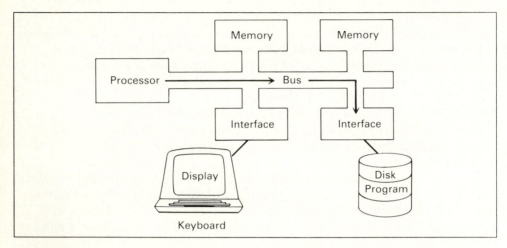

Figure 5.11 The process of loading and executing a program involves several steps. **(a)** In response to a user's request to run a program, the processor sends a signal over the bus to the disk interface.

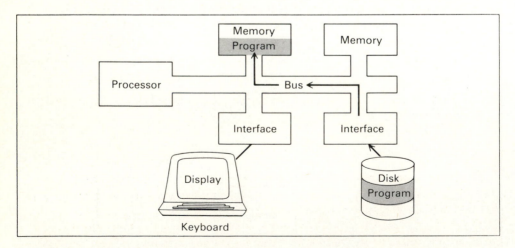

Figure 5.11(b) The program is transferred from the disk surface, through the interface, across the bus, and into memory.

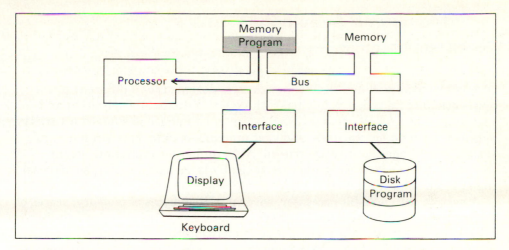

Figure 5.11(c) Once the program is in memory, the processor can execute it, fetching its instructions, one by one, over the bus.

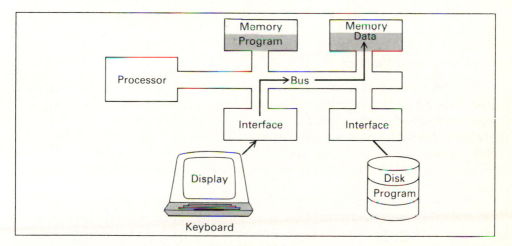

Figure 5.11(d) As the program is executed, input data move from an input device, through an interface, across the bus, and into memory.

Finally, as the program's instructions are executed, input data move from a peripheral device, over the bus, into memory (Fig. 5.11d), while output moves from memory, over the bus, and to an output device.

Note that all internal communications flow over the same bus line. Because there is only one path, the components must take turns. That limits the system's potential power. Still, single-bus architecture is a very effective way to get the job done.

Mainframe Architecture

Concurrent Processing

Because a microcomputer is designed for a single user, single-bus architecture is reasonable. A mainframe, however, is designed for a different mix of applications. Often, the system holds the organization's key operating and planning data, and all users access this central database to support a variety of tasks. With numerous users and vast amounts of data, both primary and secondary storage capacity are crucial. Also, numerous input and output devices will be needed. Programs are typically large and complex, so processing speed is important, too.

A system with a 32-bit processor, several million bytes of memory, scores of secondary storage devices, and numerous input and output devices is quite expensive, so efficiency is a key management concern. Forcing an expensive computer to wait while a human being types a line of input is not efficient. The solution is to design the system to execute several programs concurrently, with the processor switching its attention to program B while data are being input for program A. Concurrent processing will be examined in more detail in Chapter 10. Meanwhile, consider its impact on a mainframe's architecture.

Channels and Control Units

Controlling input and output involves such logical functions as selecting the path over which the data are to flow, counting characters, and computing addresses. The processor is the only source of logic on a microcomputer system, so the processor must be directly involved in each I/O operation. While it is controlling I/O, the processor is not available to execute application program instructions, but given the nature of a microcomputer system, this is a minor problem.

On a big computer supporting multiple users, it makes sense to execute several programs concurrently, but a mainframe's basic machine cycle is identical to a microcomputer's—its processor still fetches and executes one instruction at a time. How can such a machine execute two or more programs concurrently? The key is freeing the processor from responsibility for input and output. Most large systems assign the task of controlling I/O to **channels** (Fig. 5.12). A channel is a microcomputer or minicomputer with its own processor. Thus the channel's processor can perform logical functions in parallel with the computer's main processor, freeing the main processor to do other things.

A channel handles device-*independent* functions. Device-*dependent* functions such as interpreting magnetic patterns or translating internal codes to the form required by a printer are implemented through I/O **control units** or interface units (Fig. 5.13). Each physical device has its own control unit. The

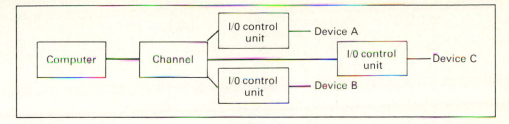

Figure 5.12 On a mainframe, device-independent functions are assigned to a channel, and device-dependent functions are assigned to an I/O control unit.

channel communicates with the computer in the computer's language; the control unit communicates with the external device on the device's terms; the channel and the control unit, working together, translate.

A typical large computer system might have three or four channels, with numerous control units attached to each one. This is a very flexible approach. It allows hundreds of input and output devices to access the computer through only a few easy-to-control data paths.

Multiple Bus Lines

A channel moves data between memory and a peripheral device. The computer's processor manipulates data in memory. Allowing a channel and a processor to access memory simultaneously won't work on a microcomputer because the single-bus architecture provides only one data path. Simultaneous operation requires independent data paths, so mainframes use **multiple-bus architecture** (Fig. 5.13).

On a typical multiple-bus machine the main processor starts an I/O operation by sending an electronic signal over the command bus to the channel (Fig. 5.13a). As program A's data move into memory over the channel's data bus (Fig. 5.13b), the processor, using its own data bus, can manipulate program B's data. When the I/O operation is finished, the channel notifies the processor by sending an electronic signal called an **interrupt** over the command bus (Fig. 5.13c). The processor can now return to program A.

Once again, when you focus on electronics, it's easy to overlook the obvious. A mainframe might support dozens of secondary storage devices and hundreds of input and output devices. If the one-slot-per-device rule were still in effect, the mainframe would have to be huge just to provide space for plugging in all those peripherals. Instead, only a few channels are directly linked to the computer. In turn, peripheral devices are plugged into the channels. This flexible design allows the same basic mainframe to support a small system or a large, multiple-channel system with hundreds of peripherals.

**Linking the Components
Mainframe Architecture**

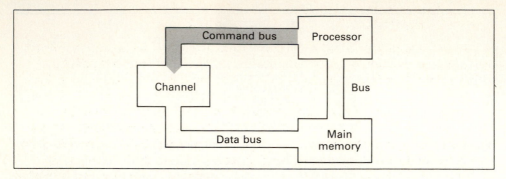

Figure 5.13 Many mainframes use multiple-bus architecture. **(a)** The main processor starts an I/O operation by sending a signal to the channel.

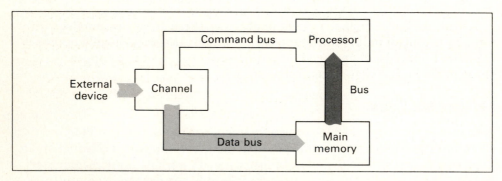

Figure 5.13(b) The channel assumes responsibility for the I/O operation, and the processor turns its attention to another program.

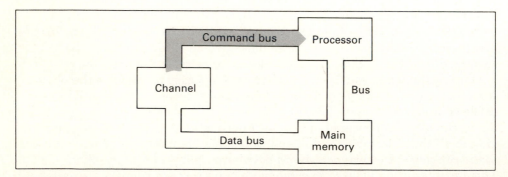

Figure 5.13(c) The channel sends an interrupt to the processor to signal the end of the I/O operation.

Summary

A computer's internal components are linked by bus lines. Peripheral devices are linked to the computer by cables. Bus lines and parallel cables move data in parallel, several bits at a time. Serial cables move data bit by bit.

On most computers the internal components are designed around a common word size. The choice of a word size affects a computer's speed, memory capacity, precision, and cost. Sometimes, memory capacity and precision can be increased by sacrificing processing speed.

A microcomputer is constructed around a metal framework called a motherboard. Features are added by plugging memory boards and various interface boards into available slots; the number of slots limits the number of peripherals that can be added. Typically, each peripheral device requires its own interface board.

Mainframes often support multiple concurrent users. Rather than wasting the main processor's time controlling input and output, the responsibility for I/O is transferred to a channel, which communicates with the computer and performs a number of device-independent functions. Those tasks depending on the external device are assigned to control units, which are plugged into the channels. Because a channel contains its own processor, it can work simultaneously with the main processor. When a channel completes an I/O operation, it notifies the main processor by sending it an interrupt.

Key Words

architecture	minicomputer
bus	motherboard
cable	multiple-bus architecture
channel	parallel
control unit	serial
interface	single-bus architecture
interrupt	slot
mainframe	word
microcomputer	

Self-Test

1. A computer's internal components are linked by ___bus lines___

2. A bus moves data in ___parallel___, several bits at a time.

3. On a ___serial___ line, the bits are transmitted one by one.

4. On most computers, all the internal components are designed around a common
   ___word size___

5. Word size affects a computer's _capacity_ , _speed_ , _word_ , and
   precision.

6. On a microcomputer system, _speed_ can be sacrificed for memory capacity.

7. Most microcomputers are constructed around a metal framework called a
   mother board

8. The number of peripherals that can be linked to a microcomputer is limited by the number of available _slots_.

9. Most microcomputers use _one-bus_ architecture.

10. On a microcomputer system, each peripheral device has its own _interface_.

11. On a microcomputer the _processor_ controls I/O.

12. On a large computer the responsibility for directly controlling I/O is often assigned to a _channel_.

13. On a large computer, functions that are unique to a given peripheral device are assigned to a _control unit_

14. Most mainframes use _multiple bus_ architecture.

15. A channel notifies the processor that an I/O operation is complete by sending an electronic signal called an _interrupt_.

Relating the Concepts

1. Distinguish between parallel and serial data transmission.

2. How are a computer's internal components physically linked?

3. On most computers, all internal components are designed around a common word size. Why?

4. Explain how a computer's word size affects its processing speed, memory capacity, and precision.

5. Distinguish between a microcomputer, a minicomputer, and a mainframe.

6. The terms motherboard, slot, and bus are used to describe a microcomputer's architecture. Relate them.

7. What does the term architecture mean when it is applied to a computer?

8. On a typical microcomputer system, each input, output, and secondary storage device has its own interface. Why?

9. Distinguish between single- and multiple-bus architecture.

10. What is a channel? What is an I/O control unit? Distinguish between the functions performed by a channel and the functions performed by an I/O control unit.

6

Microcomputer Operating Systems

Preview

A computer's operating system serves as the interface between hardware and software. This chapter describes the major components of a typical, single-user microcomputer operating system. Key concepts include:

The hardware/software interface

Communicating with the operating system

- The command language

Accessing peripherals

- Primitive commands

- The input/output control system

Loading the operating system

Some examples

The Hardware/Software Interface

When you think of software, you probably visualize **application programs** that support such end-user tasks as playing a game, writing a paper, creating a spreadsheet,

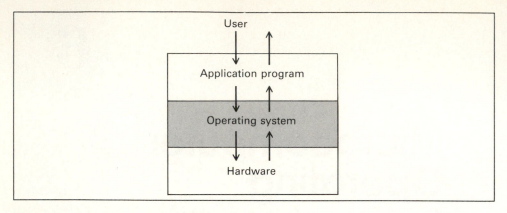

Figure 6.1 The operating system serves as an interface between hardware and application software.

or generating paychecks. Another type of software, called **system software**, performs its assigned tasks behind the scenes. An excellent example is the **operating system** found on most computers. An operating system serves as an interface (Fig. 6.1), bridging the gap between hardware and application software.

An operating system performs a number of support functions. For example, picture an application program stored on disk. Before the program can be executed, it must first be copied into memory. The process of copying a program from disk to memory involves considerable logic. The source of a computer's logic is software, so if the application program is to be loaded, there must be a program in memory to control the loading process. That program is the operating system.

Loading programs is just one of the operating system's many support functions. Basically, the operating system is a collection of software modules that insulate the user from the hardware, making the system easier to use.

Communicating with the Operating System

Computers are not intelligent. Before the operating system can perform one of its support functions, the person using the computer must tell it what to do. The user, much like a military officer, issues orders. The operating system responds like a sergeant, gathering the necessary resources and carrying out each command. The operating system module that accepts, interprets, and carries out commands is the **command processor** (Fig. 6.2).

The command processor consists of a number of routines, each of which performs a single task (Fig. 6.3). For example, one module contains the instructions that guide the computer through the process of copying a program from disk and loading it into memory. Another module contains the instructions that transfer control of the computer to that program.

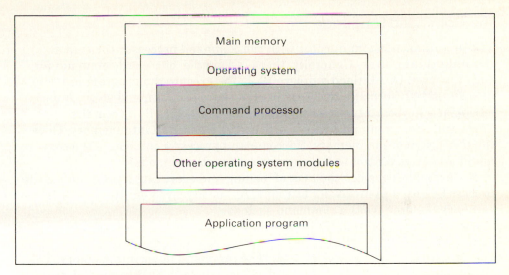

Figure 6.2 The operating system module that accepts, interprets, and carries out commands is called the command processor.

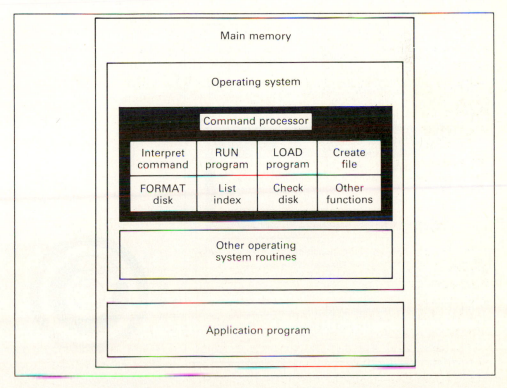

Figure 6.3 The command processor is composed of a number of program modules, each of which performs a single logical function.

The Command Language

The programmer communicates with the command processor through a **command language**. Generally, there is a simple, one-word command for each function: LOAD (load a program), RUN (execute the program in memory), FORMAT (format a disk), DISKCOPY (copy a disk), and so on. A user sitting at a keyboard types a command. The characters flow from the keyboard, through an interface board, across a bus, and into memory. Once the characters are in memory, the command processor interprets the command and gives control to the appropriate functional module.

For example, consider the task of loading and executing a program. As the process begins, a **prompt** (for example, A>) is displayed on the screen. In response the user types a command such as

    LOAD MYPGM

and presses the enter key (Fig. 6.4a). The command flows into memory. The command processor evaluates it, and, recognizing a LOAD command, transfers control to the program loading module (Fig. 6.4b), which reads the

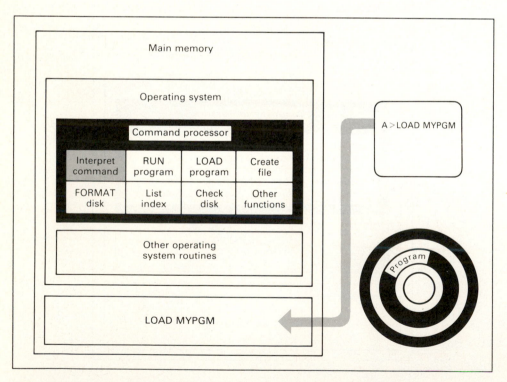

Figure 6.4 The operating system is responsible for loading an application program and giving it control. **(a)** Responding to the operating system's prompt, a user types a load command. The command processor then interprets the command.

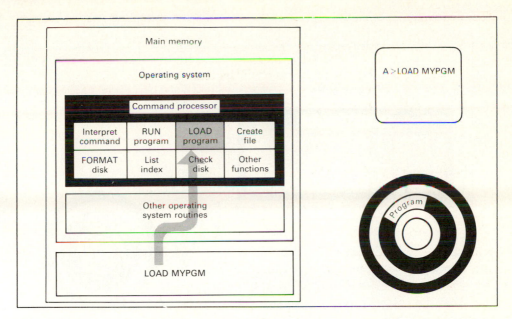

Figure 6.4(b) The command says to load a program, so the command processor's program loading module gets control.

requested program from disk into memory. Once the program is loaded, the command processor gets control again, displays another prompt, and waits for the next command (Fig. 6.4c).

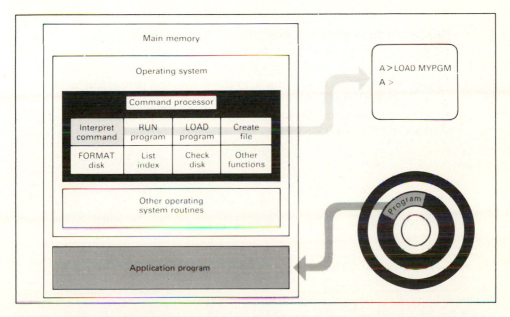

Figure 6.4(c) After the program is loaded, the command processor gets control, displays its prompt, and waits for the next command.

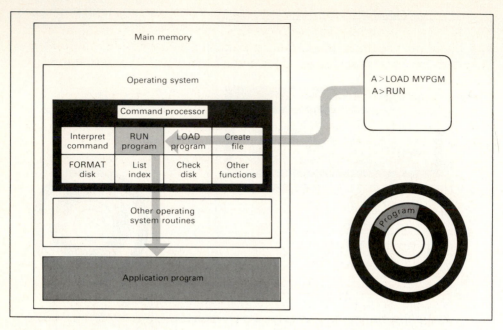

Figure 6.4(d) The next command tells the operating system to run the program in memory, so the command processor gives control to the module that starts the application program.

The next command is

RUN

It tells the operating system to execute the program stored in memory. Following a RUN command, the command processor gives control to the module that starts the application program (Fig. 6.4d). When the program is finished executing, it gives control back to the command processor, which displays a prompt and waits for the next command.

On most microcomputers the command processor is the operating system's main control module (Fig. 6.5), accepting commands, interpreting them, and

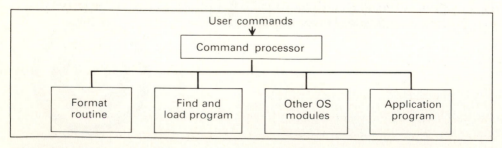

Figure 6.5 Most microcomputer operating systems are command driven.

determining which lower-level modules are needed to carry them out. Those modules communicate directly with the hardware. When they are done, the modules return control to the command processor, which displays a prompt and waits for the next command. Such systems are said to be **command driven**.

The command processor is sometimes called the **shell**. Because it represents the user's primary interface with the system, the shell defines an operating environment. For example, many users find the cryptic commands associated with most microcomputer operating systems confusing. If the traditional shell is replaced by a more user-friendly interface, users might issue commands by selecting them from a menu or by pointing to a graphic icon.

Accessing Peripherals

Primitive Commands

One of the modules described in the previous section "finds and loads" a program. The explanation glossed over several details. There is some logic involved in finding and loading a program.

For example, assume that the program is stored on disk. A disk drive contains little or no intelligence; it is limited to performing certain primitive operations, including:

1. Seek to a selected track.

2. Read a selected sector from that track.

3. Write a selected sector to that track.

That's it. That is all a disk drive can do. The only way to read a program from disk into memory is to send the drive a series of **primitive commands** asking it to seek and read, one by one, each sector that holds part of the program. Note that the disk drive must be told exactly where to position the read/write mechanism and exactly which sectors to read.

Imagine having to communicate with the system at a primitive level. If a program were stored on track 20, sectors 8 and 9, you would have to tell the system to:

```
SEEK 20
READ 8
SEEK 20
READ 9
```

Of course, it would be your responsibility to remember that the program is stored on track 20, sectors 8 and 9. What if you forgot? Chances are you would never see your program again.

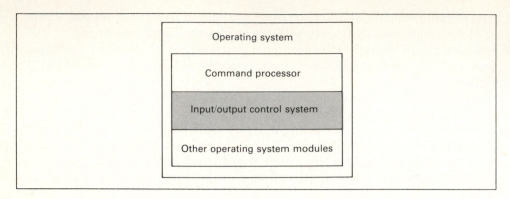

Figure 6.6 Most operating systems also contain an input-output control system. The IOCS is the module that communicates directly with the peripheral equipment.

The Input/Output Control System

What does the user want? A specific program. Does the user really care where that program is physically stored? Probably not. The typical user simply wants the program; the primitive hardware details associated with finding and loading it are (or should be) the computer's concern. This is where the operating system comes into play. Most contain an **input/output control system**, or **IOCS** (Fig. 6.6), that generates the necessary primitive commands.

Imagine that a program named SPACEWAR is stored on track 20, sector 8. Which do you find easier to remember—Track 20, sector 8 or SPACEWAR? Most people think of programs by name. The purpose of an operating system is to insulate the user from the hardware—to make the hardware easier to use. Since people find it easy to remember programs by name, it makes sense to design the input/output control system to accept a name and translate it to physical commands.

You learned in Chapter 4 that the various programs stored on a disk are listed in the disk's directory (Fig. 6.7). The directory is the key to accessing programs by name. For example, following the command

        LOAD SPACEWAR

the command processor transfers control to the program loading module. That module in turn calls on the input/output control system, which reads the directory. Once the directory is in memory, the IOCS can search it. Each program on the disk is identified by name; note that SPACEWAR is the third entry. Following the program's name is its disk address. Using this information, the IOCS issues the seek and read commands that copy the program into memory.

When a program is first written to disk, its name and disk address are recorded in the directory. To retrieve the program, the directory is read and

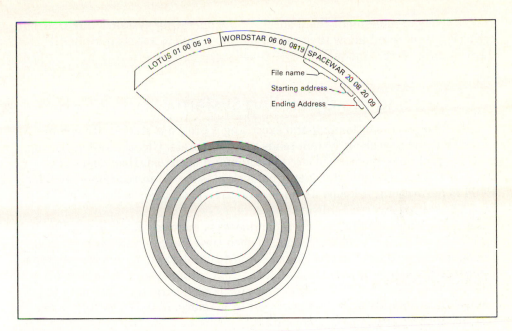

Figure 6.7 The directory found on each disk is the key to accessing programs by name.

searched for the program name, the program's address is extracted from the directory, and the necessary primitive I/O commands are issued. The input/output control system manages the directory and generates the primitive commands.

This example was based on accessing disk. The IOCS is responsible for communicating with the system's other peripheral devices, too. Each physical device is controlled by its own unique set of primitive commands. (Incidentally, that's another reason why each input or output device requires its own interface or control unit.) Application programs issue general requests to start input or to start output. The input/output control system accepts these general requests and generates the primitive commands needed to control a specific peripheral device.

Establishing communication with an external device involves more than just generating primitive commands, however. For example, whenever two hardware components (such as a computer and a disk drive) communicate with each other, their electronic signals must be carefully synchronized. Synchronization involves exchanging a predetermined set of signals called a **protocol**. Starting or checking protocol signals is a tedious process that is usually assigned to the operating system.

The process of starting, ending, and controlling any input or output operation involves a surprising number of technical details. Rather than duplicating the logic to perform these functions in every application program, it makes sense to implement them once—in the operating system's input/output control system—and allow the application programs to access peripheral devices through this module.

Loading the Operating System

The process of loading and executing a program starts with a command that the operating system reads and interprets. Clearly, the operating system must be in memory before the command is issued. How does it get there? On a few systems the operating system is stored in read-only memory. ROM is permanent; it keeps its contents even when power is lost. A ROM-based operating system is always there.

However, most computers use random access memory. RAM is volatile. It loses its contents when power is cut, so each time the computer is activated, the operating system must be loaded. Unfortunately, you cannot simply type a command, such as LOAD OS, and let the operating system take care of loading itself. Why not? When the computer is first turned on, memory is empty. If the operating system is not yet in memory, it can't possibly read, interpret, and carry out the command.

Typically, the operating system is stored on disk. The idea is to copy it into memory. This objective is achieved by a special program called a **boot** (Fig. 6.8). The boot routine is stored on the first sector (or two) of a disk. Hardware is designed to read this sector automatically whenever the power is turned on (Fig. 6.8a). The boot consists of only a few instructions, but they are sufficient to read the rest of the operating system into memory (Fig. 6.8b). Note how the boot is seemingly "pulled in by its own bootstraps." Now a user can type the commands to load and execute an application program.

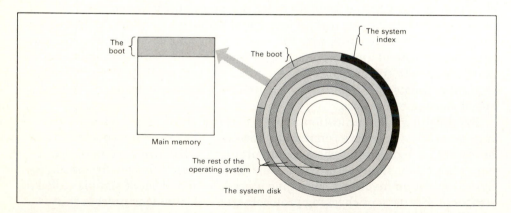

Figure 6.8 The operating system is loaded into memory by a special program called the boot. **(a)** When the computer is first turned on, hardware automatically reads the boot program from the first few sectors of a disk.

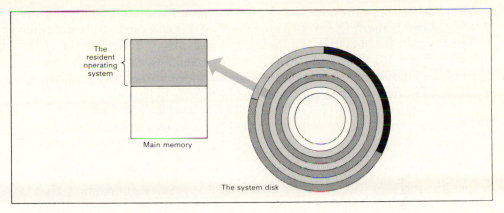

Figure 6.8(b) The boot routine contains the instructions that read the rest of the operating system from disk into memory.

Some Examples

At the hardware level, computers made by different manufacturers are often incompatible, so a program written for one won't work on another. Remember, however, that the operating system sits between the hardware and the application program. With a common operating system in the middle, it is possible for the same program to run on two quite different machines (Fig. 6.9). Of course, the portions of the operating system that communicate with the hardware might be very different, but software would see a smooth, common interface. Consequently, a standard operating system promotes software compatibility between computers from different suppliers.

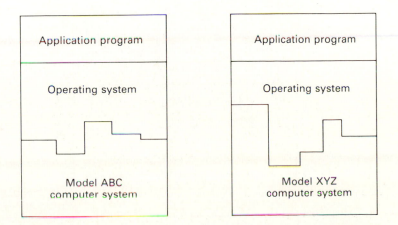

Figure 6.9 The operating system presents the application program with a smooth, consistent interface.

MS/DOS, perhaps the best known microcomputer operating system, was developed by Microsoft Corporation for the IBM-PC and compatible machines and has become an industry standard. It is composed of three primary modules (Fig. 6.10). COMMAND.COM is the command processor. The functions of the input/output control system are divided between two routines, MSDOS.SYS and IO.SYS. MSDOS.SYS is hardware-independent. IO.SYS, on the other hand, communicates directly with the hardware and contains device-dependent code. Versions of the operating system written for different computers should differ only in their IO.SYS logic. In addition to the primary modules, MS/DOS contains several utility programs.

When MS/DOS is booted, COMMAND.COM, MSDOS.SYS, and IO.SYS are copied into memory. The transient area (Fig. 6.10) consists of memory that is not assigned to the operating system. Application programs, system utilities, certain transient modules, and data are read into the transient area.

Because MS/DOS is so widely used, a vast library of application software has been developed for it. This software library will tend to perpetuate

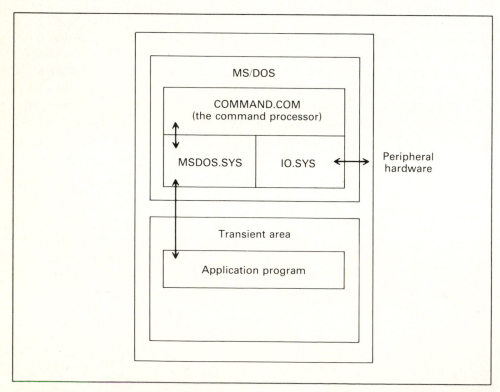

Figure 6.10 MS/DOS, perhaps the best-known microcomputer operating system, is composed of three primary modules.

MS/DOS's status as a standard simply because it makes sense to buy a computer for which software already exists. Virtually every significant microcomputer supplier supports MS/DOS, at least as an option.

MS/DOS commands are rather cryptic, and beginners often find them frustrating. Fortunately, custom shells are commercially available. For example, Microsoft Windows defines a graphic interface that allows a user to issue MS/DOS commands by pointing to icons.

As microcomputer technology continues to improve, operating systems designed to take advantage of the newer, more powerful machines are beginning to challenge MS/DOS. For example, OS/2 was created to support IBM's PS/2 computer series. It can run virtually all MS/DOS programs. Additionally, it can utilize extended memory and run two or more programs concurrently.

UNIX, a product of AT&T, shows promise of becoming a new standard, particularly for applications involving data communication and networks. Originally designed to be an effective program development environment, UNIX is now available on a variety of computers, including microcomputers. Because the operating system runs on many different machines, UNIX programs are highly portable. Additionally, UNIX contains features common to most mainframe operating systems. Those advanced features will be covered in Chapter 10.

Summary

An operating system is a collection of modules that serve as a hardware/software interface. Users communicate with the operating system through a command language. The command processor accepts, interprets, and carries out the commands. Most microcomputer operating systems are command driven. The command processor, sometimes called a shell, defines an operating environment.

Communicating with input and output devices is difficult because each is controlled by its own primitive commands. The input/output control system (IOCS) accepts requests for I/O and generates the necessary primitives. Maintaining disk directories is a key IOCS task. Another function of the IOCS is generating and interpreting the protocol signals that are needed to synchronize devices before they begin to communicate.

Because a computer's main memory is volatile, the operating system must be loaded each time the computer is turned on. The routine that loads the operating system is called a boot. Typically stored on the first sector or two of a disk, the boot is read by hardware. Once in memory, it loads the rest of the operating system.

A common operating system allows a given program to run on different computers. Perhaps the best-known microcomputer operating system is

MS/DOS. Microsoft Windows is a popular MS/DOS shell. OS/2 was developed to support IBM's new PS/2 series. UNIX shows promise of becoming a new standard.

Key Words

application program	operating system
boot	primitive command
command driven	prompt
command language	protocol
command processor	shell
input/output control system (IOCS)	system software
MS/DOS	

Self-Test

1. The _____ serves as a hardware/software interface.

2. _____ is the source of a computer's logic.

3. The operating system module that accepts, interprets, and carries out commands is the _____

4. A user communicates with the operating system through a _____.

5. Most microcomputer operating systems are _____ driven. The command processor, sometimes called a _____, defines an operating environment.

6. A disk drive is physically controlled by _____

7. The operating system module that sends primitive commands to the disk drive is the _____.

8. The name and location of each program stored on a disk is found on the disk's _____

9. The _____ is responsible for communicating with all peripheral devices.

10. Before two devices can communicate, they must synchronize by exchanging _____ signals.

11. _____ is permanent; _____ is volatile.

12. The operating system is loaded by a _____ routine.

13. The best-known microcomputer operating system is probably _____.

14. _____ shows promise of becoming a new standard, particularly for applications involving communication and networks.

15. _____ was developed to support IBM's new PS/2 series.

Relating the Concepts

1. Distinguish between application programs and system software.

2. An operating system serves as an interface between application programs and hardware. Explain.

3. What does the operating system's command processor do? Relate the command processor to its command language.

4. What does the operating system's input/output control system do?

5. What are primitive commands? Why are they necessary?

6. Imagine that a program named MYPGM is stored on disk. Briefly explain how the operating system loads it into main memory. Start with the user's command.

7. Explain how an operating system is booted. Why is booting necessary?

8. Sketch the component parts of a microcomputer operating system. Briefly explain what each component does.

9. Sketch the component parts of MS/DOS. Compare its components to the ones you sketched for Exercise 8.

10. A standard operating system promotes software compatibility. Why is this important?

7

Application Software

Preview

A computer can do nothing without a program to provide control. Most people access the computer under the control of an application program. This chapter briefly describes the process of writing an application program and then introduces several popular commercially available programs. Key concepts include:

Writing programs

- Instructions
- Planning the program's logic
- Machine and assembler language
- Compilers and interpreters
- Nonprocedural languages

Artificial intelligence

- Natural language processing
- Expert systems
- Fifth-generation machines

Commercial software

The user interface

Writing Programs

Instructions

A **program** is a series of **instructions** that guides a computer through a process. Each instruction tells the machine to perform one of its basic functions: add, subtract, multiply, divide, compare, copy, start input, or start output. A typical instruction (Fig. 7.1) begins with an operation code that specifies the function to be performed. Next come one or more operands that identify the data to be manipulated. For example, the instruction

```
ADD  3,4
```

tells a hypothetical computer to add the contents of registers 3 and 4.

Because a computer's instruction set is limited, even simple logical operations call for several instructions. For example, imagine two data values stored in memory. To add them, both values must first be loaded into registers. The registers are then added, and the answer is stored back into memory. That's four instructions just to add two values: LOAD, LOAD, ADD, and STORE. Imagine the number of instructions in a sophisticated program.

Planning the Program's Logic

Programs do not simply spring into being; they are written by people called programmers. Because computers have little tolerance for error, the programmer must define the *right* instructions in the right sequence. The starting point is a user who needs information; the desired information represents the program's output (Fig. 7.2). The next step in planning the program is to define the **algorithms** or sets of rules needed to generate that output. Finally, the required input data are identified. Given the necessary input, the algorithms, and the desired output, the programmer knows what the program must do.

The inputs, the algorithms, and the outputs might be enough for a simple program, but complex programs require additional planning. The process of planning a major program is outlined in Chapter 9. Given an acceptable plan, the programmer can begin to translate the data descriptions and the algorithms into a series of instructions using a programming language. The finished program tells the computer how to obtain the desired output.

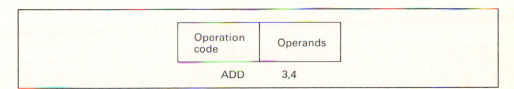

Figure 7.1 An instruction is composed of an operation code and one or more operands. The operation code tells the computer what to do. The operand or operands specify the addresses of the data elements to be manipulated.

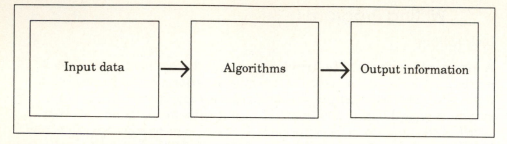

Figure 7.2 The first step in planning a program is to identify the desired output, the algorithms needed to generate that output, and the input data that drive those algorithms.

Machine and Assembler Language

A computer is controlled by a program stored in its own memory. Because memory stores bits, the program must be in binary form. Figure 7.3 shows the binary **machine language** instructions needed to add two numbers on a typical mainframe computer.

Second-generation **assembler** languages were a significant improvement over machine language. An assembler programmer writes one mnemonic (memory-aiding) statement for each machine-level instruction. For example, Fig. 7.4 shows an assembler language routine to add two numbers.

There are no computers that directly execute assembler language instructions. Writing mnemonic codes might simplify the programmer's job, but computers are still binary machines and require binary instructions, so translation is necessary. An assembler program (Fig. 7.4) reads a programmer's **source code**, translates each source statement to a single binary instruction, and produces an **object module**. Because the object

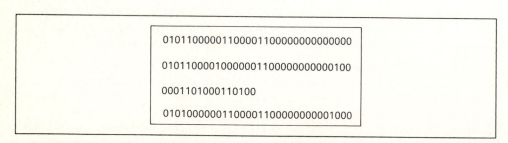

Figure 7.3 Because a computer's main memory stores bits, the program must exist in binary form. These four instructions add two numbers on an IBM mainframe computer.

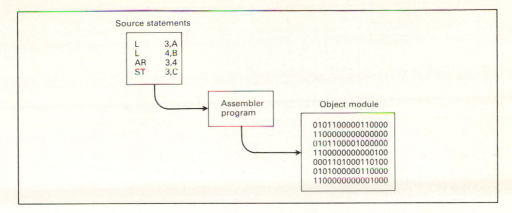

Figure 7.4 An assembler reads a programmer's mnemonic source statements, translates each one to a single machine-level instruction, and then combines them to form an object module.

module is a machine-level version of the programmer's code, it can be executed.

Compilers and Interpreters

A computer needs four machine-level instructions to add two numbers because that is the way a computer works. Human beings should not have to think like computers. For example, one way to view addition is as an algebraic expression:

    C = A + B

Why not allow a programmer to write something like algebraic expressions, read those source statements into a program, and have the program generate the necessary machine-level code?

That's exactly what happens with a **compiler** (Fig. 7.5). Many compiler languages, including FORTRAN, BASIC, Pascal, and PL/1, are algebraically based. Statements in COBOL, the most popular business-oriented language, resemble English sentences (Fig. 7.6). Compilers represent software's third generation.

The difference between an assembler and a compiler is subtle. With an assembler, each source statement is converted to a *single* machine-level instruction. With a compiler a given source statement is converted to one or more (usually, more) machine-level instructions. An option is using an **interpreter**. Assemblers and compilers read a complete source program and generate a complete object module. An interpreter, on the other hand, works with one source statement at a time, reading it, translating it to machine-level, executing the resulting binary instructions, and then moving on to the next source statement.

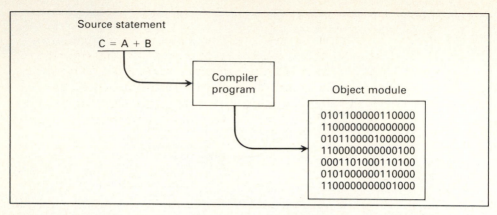

Source statement

C = A + B

Compiler program

Object module

0101100000110000
1100000000000000
0101100001000000
1100000000000100
0001101000110100
0101000000110000
1100000000001000

Figure 7.5 A compiler reads the programmer's source statements, translates each one to one or more machine-level instructions, and then combines them to form an object module.

Each programming language has its own syntax; for example, a Pascal source program is meaningless to a COBOL compiler or a BASIC interpreter. However, no matter what language is used, the objective is the same. An assembler program accepts mnemonic source code and generates a machine-level object module. A FORTRAN compiler accepts FORTRAN source code and generates a machine-level object module. A COBOL compiler accepts COBOL source code and generates a machine-level object module.

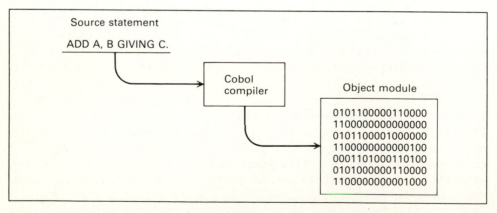

Source statement

ADD A, B GIVING C.

Cobol compiler

Object module

0101100000110000
1100000000000000
0101100001000000
1100000000000100
0001101000110100
0101000000110000
1100000000001000

Figure 7.6 The most popular business-oriented language is COBOL.

Nonprocedural Languages

With traditional assemblers, compilers, and interpreters the programmer defines a procedure to tell the computer how to solve a problem. However, with a modern **nonprocedural language** (sometimes called a fourth-generation or declarative language) the programmer simply defines the logical structure of the problem and lets the language translator figure out how to solve it. Examples of commercially available nonprocedural languages include Prolog, Focus, and many others.

Artificial Intelligence

Natural Language Processing

The machine language programmer almost literally had to "think" like a computer. With an assembler the programmer writes mnemonic codes rather than binary instructions. A compiler source program specifies an algorithm in almost human terms. With a nonprocedural language the computer assumes much of the responsibility for defining the program's logical flow. Note that in moving from the first to the fourth generation, the amount of machine-specific detail expected from the programmer steadily declines (Fig. 7.7).

If only a computer could think like a human being, the problem of telling it what to do (or programming it) would be greatly simplified. The idea of a thinking machine belongs more to science fiction than to science, but it might be possible to create a friendly interface that allows a person to communicate

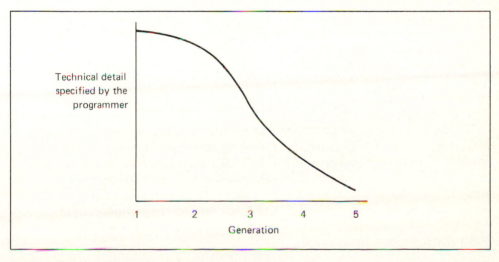

Figure 7.7 As programming languages evolved, the amount of machine-specific detail specified by the programmer declined.

with the machine in human terms. The computer could then assume responsibility for translating human language into "computerese," a process almost exactly opposite that followed by a first-generation programmer. Picture Mr. Spock talking to the computer on the starship Enterprise, and you have a good mental image of how a fifth-generation language might work.

Natural language processing is a major area of research within the broader field of **artificial intelligence**, and developing a friendly, human-like interface is one of its key objectives. With such a friendly interface between the programmer and the computer, automatic program generation becomes feasible. In effect, the human being will be able to specify *what* must be done, and the computer will determine *how* to do it.

Unfortunately, natural language processing is not that simple. Human language is imprecise; even the most everyday conversations are loaded with subtle shades of meaning. Add the incredible variety of languages, dialects, and accents, and you have a very complex problem. Additionally, few people are skilled at issuing orders or precisely specifying their needs. For example, when things get serious on board the Enterprise, it's always Spock who talks to the computer. He is precise, but then he's only half human.

Full natural language processing is not yet commercially available, but considerable research is being conducted in laboratories throughout the world. Natural language processing has tremendous potential.

Expert Systems

No discussion of artificial intelligence would be complete without at least a brief introduction to **expert systems**, which *are* commercially available. In fact, people who are unfamiliar with the field sometimes consider artificial intelligence and expert systems to be synonymous.

Mycin, a medical diagnosis routine, is a well known expert system. Given a description of a patient's symptoms, it suggests a surprisingly accurate diagnosis and treatment. Mycin is particularly useful in remote areas where human expertise is not available. Geologists use expert systems to extract patterns from satellite photos and other data. The military uses expert systems to support a ship's tactical officer and to guide "smart" weapons. Many other examples could be cited.

Traditional computer programs follow algorithms, or well-defined rules, but people often think heuristically, relying on rules of thumb, inferences, and intelligent trial and error. Thus the task of creating an expert system begins with a human expert. Through interviews and observation of the expert in action, the decision-making process is carefully documented. Finally, the process is translated into terms a computer can understand.

Fifth-Generation Machines

Most existing computers are designed to perform calculations; they are at their best when adding, subtracting, multiplying, and dividing. Artificial intelligence relies more on symbolic reasoning. Consequently, current computers are far from ideal. The solution might be to build a new type of computer designed specifically with symbolic reasoning in mind. Much current research, particularly in Japan, is directed at creating just such a machine. Some experts even look beyond the fifth generation and envision sixth-generation machines based on dense, parallel neural nets that simulate the human brain.

Commercial Software

Relatively few people actually write original programs. Instead, most access the computer through such **commercial software** packages as spreadsheets, word processors, database managers, accounting programs, and so on. These ready-to-use programs are sold much like sound recordings; a consumer purchases a copy on disk, loads it onto his or her computer, and uses the software.

Word processing software simplifies the task of writing text (Fig. 7.8). On a superficial level the computer becomes a replacement for a typewriter, but there is more to writing than just mechanics. The secret to quality writing is to revise and rewrite material several times. A word processor supports document revision by making it easy to delete, insert, and move words, sentences, paragraphs, and even large blocks of text. Most word processors include a spelling checker and a thesaurus, and some can even

```
                    Howard and Johnson, Ltd.
                    "Creativity is Our Thing!"
                          P.O. Box Z
                       Oxford, Ohio 01056

                                              January 22, 1991


Ms. Charlie Angel
Program Director
CBS Television
New York, New York  10001

Dear Ms. Angel:

Mary Howard and Hector Johnson, two of the most creative minds in
television today, have been responsible for such hits as "Bleep the
Boss" and "Humiliate Your Spouse." Graduates of the South Dakota
School of Broadcasting, this incredible team has been a gold mine
of original hits since 1988.

Today, Howard and Johnson are proud to announce the development of
their newest mega-hit, "The Betagosa Hillbillies." Please see the
attached press release for details.

                             Doc 1 Pg 1 Ln 1" Pos 1"
```

Figure 7.8 A word processing program simplifies the task of writing text.

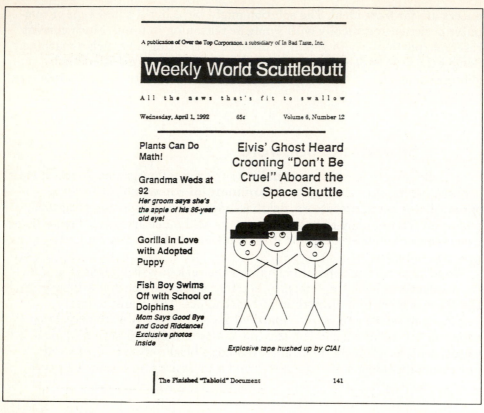

Figure 7.9 Desktop publishing software generates output that resembles set type.

identify style problems. Efficient mail merge routines are another common feature.

Much of this book was written using WordPerfect, a popular word processing program. Major competitors include DisplayWrite, Microsoft Word, Multimate, Wordstar, and many others. **Desktop publishing** is a step beyond word processing. Programs such as PageMaker and Ventura Publisher allow a user to lay out the contents of a page, integrate text and graphics, and generate a document that resembles set type (Fig. 7.9). Some advanced word processors incorporate desktop publishing features.

An **electronic spreadsheet** program called Visicalc was the first commercially significant microcomputer application. An accountant's spreadsheet is a piece of paper with horizontal and vertical lines dividing it into rows and columns; the software allows a user to simulate a spreadsheet on the screen (Fig. 7.10). Lotus 1-2-3 is today's biggest selling electronic spreadsheet; key competitors include Excel, Quattro, and Supercalc.

Database management is another significant microcomputer application. Database software is concerned with the efficient storage and retrieval

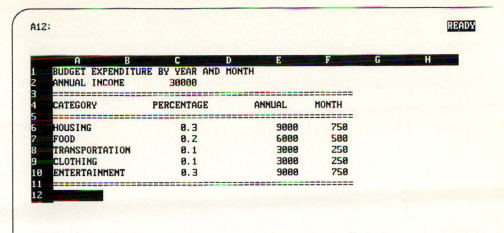

```
        A       B       C       D       E       F       G       H
1   BUDGET EXPENDITURE BY YEAR AND MONTH
2   ANNUAL INCOME        30000
3   ===================================================================
4   CATEGORY        PERCENTAGE          ANNUAL      MONTH
5   ===================================================================
6   HOUSING             0.3              9000        750
7   FOOD                0.2              6000        500
8   TRANSPORTATION      0.1              3000        250
9   CLOTHING            0.1              3000        250
10  ENTERTAINMENT       0.3              9000        750
11  ===================================================================
12
```

Figure 7.10 Spreadsheet software simulates an accountant's spreadsheet on the screen.

of data, and most packages include facilities to assemble reports quickly (Fig. 7.11). Popular database programs include dBASE III Plus, dBASE IV, R Base, Reflex, and many others.

```
                CAMPUS THREADS DEPOSITS BY DORMITORY

Page No.    1
03/06/91

FIRST_NAME      LAST_NAME           ROOM  DORMITORY              DEPOSIT

FRODO           BAGGINS             105   BAG END HALL            40.00
BILBO           BAGGINS             105   BAG END HALL            30.00

** Subtotal **                                                   70.00

ARAGORN         STRIDER             400   BRANDYWINE HALL         50.00

** Subtotal **                                                   50.00

THORIN          OAKENSHIELD         113   ELROND HOUSE            90.00

** Subtotal **                                                   90.00

LISA            KALO                108   EMERISON HALL           50.00

** Subtotal **                                                   50.00
```

Figure 7.11 Most database management systems can generate sophisticated reports.

Application Software
Commercial Software

Accounting software is a big seller in the business world. Programs to perform such tasks as payroll, accounts receivable, accounts payable, general ledger, inventory, and many others are commercially available. Some packages are generic; payroll is, after all, payroll. Others are more specialized, providing the programs needed to run a dental practice, a construction firm, or some other organization. In technical firms, computer-aided design/computer-aided manufacturing (CAD/CAM) programs have become almost the standard for preparing engineering drawings.

The User Interface

As the user of an application routine, your link to the computer will be through the software's **user interface**. Some programs are designed to respond to **commands**; others display a **menu** of commands or options and invite the user to select one. Sometimes the menu choices are presented as pictures or icons.

Menu-driven software (Fig. 7.12) is relatively easy to learn because all possible choices are displayed on the screen. The menu supports a "point and select" mode of operation that is particularly convenient when the system is equipped with a mouse. The problem with menus is that they sometimes get in the way. As you begin to learn how to use a program, the sequence of steps required to perform a common function eventually becomes almost second nature, and working through a series of menus can become annoying.

Experienced users tend to favor command-driven software (Fig. 7.13) because all the steps required to perform even a complex function can often be typed on a single line or quickly issued by pressing a series of function keys. Unfortunately, beginners sometimes struggle with command-driven

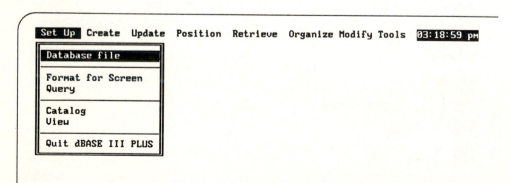

Figure 7.12 A typical menu.

```
. FIND BAGGINS
. DISPLAY FIELDS LAST_NAME, FIRST_NAME
Record#  LAST_NAME            FIRST_NAME
    11   BAGGINS              BILBO
.
```

| Command Line | <B:> CUSTOMER | Rec: 11/26 | Caps |

Enter a dBASE III PLUS command.

Figure 7.13 Some programs are driven by user commands.

programs because several commands might be required to perform even the most elementary task.

Recognizing the limitations of both approaches, the designers of many software packages give you a choice. For example, Lotus 1-2-3 is menu driven (Fig. 7.14), but you can select a command from the menu by typing the first letter of the command name. dBASE III Plus allows the user to work through a series of menus or to issue commands in "dot prompt" mode. WordPerfect is command driven with the commands issued by pressing function keys, but the latest version of WordPerfect includes an optional menu interface, too.

Another common feature of many popular application programs is the use of **windows** to display error messages and secondary menus (Fig. 7.15). A window is a small box that displays a message on a portion of the screen, leaving much of the original screen visible in the background. Windows allow the program to communicate with the user without breaking the link to the primary task.

```
A12:                                                                  MENU
Worksheet  Range  Copy  Move  File  Print  Graph  Data  System  Add-In  Quit
Global  Insert  Delete  Column  Erase  Titles  Window  Status  Page  Learn
         A         B         C         D         E         F         G         H
 1   BUDGET EXPENDITURE BY YEAR AND MONTH
 2   ANNUAL INCOME          30000
 3   ===================================================================
 4   CATEGORY          PERCENTAGE          ANNUAL    MONTHLY
 5   ===================================================================
 6   HOUSING              0.3                9000      750
 7   FOOD                 0.2                6000      500
 8   TRANSPORTATION       0.1                3000      250
 9   CLOTHING             0.1                3000      250
10   ENTERTAINMENT        0.3                9000      750
11   ===================================================================
12
```

Figure 7.14 Lotus 1-2-3 is menu driven, but you can select a choice from the menu by typing the first letter of the command name.

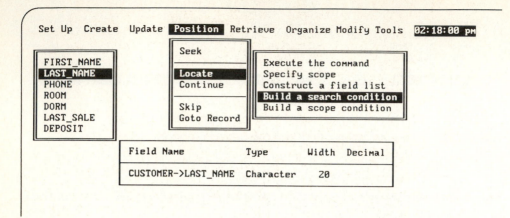

Figure 7.15 Error messages and menus are sometimes displayed in a window.

Summary

A program is a series of instructions that guides a computer through a process. Each instruction tells the machine to perform one of its basic functions. A programmer plans a program by defining the necessary outputs, the algorithms, and the inputs and then translating them into computer terms by coding them in a programming language.

A computer executes binary, machine-level instructions. An assembler language programmer writes one mnemonic instruction for each machine-level instruction; an assembler program then reads the source statements and generates a binary object module. A compiler reads source statements, translates each statement into one or more machine-level instructions, and combines them to form an object module. An interpreter works with one source statement at a time, translating it and executing the resulting machine-level code before moving on to the next instruction. A programmer using a nonprocedural, fourth-generation language defines the problem's logical structure and lets the translator program figure out how to solve it.

Many experts predict that fifth-generation languages will incorporate artificial intelligence, with natural language processing supporting a friendly, humanlike interface between the programmer and the machine. Expert systems represent one area of artificial intelligence that is already commercially available.

Few computer users write original programs. A word processor simplifies the task of writing text. An electronic spreadsheet simulates an accountant's spreadsheet on the computer. Database management software is concerned with data storage and retrieval. Accounting packages are available to perform many common business tasks.

The user's link to the computer is through the program's user interface. Some programs are command driven; others allow the user to select commands from a menu. Error messages and secondary commands are often displayed in windows.

Key Words

algorithm	machine language
artificial intelligence	menu
assembler	natural language processing
command	nonprocedural language
commercial software	object module
compiler	program
database management	source code
desktop publishing	spreadsheet, electronic
expert system	user interface
instruction	window
interpreter	word processing

Self-Test

1. In an instruction the _____ specifies the operation to be performed, while the _____ identify the data that are to be manipulated.

2. A programmer defines the _____ or rules for solving a problem and then uses a program language to translate them into "computerese."

3. The program that controls a computer must be stored in main memory in _____ form.

4. An _____ programmer writes one source instruction for each machine-level instruction.

5. Programmers write _____ code. Compilers and assemblers read a programmer's code and generate an _____.

6. A _____ translates each source statement to one or more machine-level instructions. An _____ reads a single source statement, immediately translates it to machine-level code, and then executes it before reading the next source statement.

7. With a _____ the programmer simply defines the logical structure of a problem.

8. Fifth-generation languages may incorporate _____.

9. Within the broader discipline of artificial intelligence, _____ may support user-friendly, almost human interfaces to a computer.

10. _____ represent the most successful subset of artificial intelligence.

11. A _____ simplifies the task of writing text.

12. A _____ program allows you to lay out the contents of a page and integrate text and graphics.

13. The first commercially successful spreadsheet program was _____. Today's best-selling spreadsheet program is _____.

14. _____ is concerned with the efficient storage and retrieval of data.

15. Experienced users tend to favor _____ software, while most beginners prefer to select commands from a _____.

Relating the Concepts

1. Without a program to provide control, a computer is little more than an expensive calculator. Do you agree? Why or why not?

2. Relate machine-level instructions to a computer's basic machine cycle.

3. Why are programming languages necessary?

4. Distinguish between an assembler and a compiler. Distinguish between a compiler and an interpreter.

5. Distinguish between a source module and an object module.

6. As programming languages evolved, the programmer had to worry less and less about *how* the problem would be solved on the computer. Why is that significant?

7. In your view, how will natural language processing and artificial intelligence affect programming?

8. Spreadsheets can be done by hand. What is the advantage of using a computer?

9. Text can be prepared on a typewriter. What is the advantage of using a computer and a word processor?

10. Briefly distinguish between command-driven and menu-driven user interfaces. What are the advantages and disadvantages of each?

8

Data Management

Preview

The three elements that must be present in any computer application are hardware, software, and data. This chapter introduces several data fundamentals. Key concepts include:

Why data management?

Accessing data

- Data structures
- Locating files
- Locating records
- The relative record concept

Access techniques

- Sequential access
- Direct access
- Access methods

Database management

- Why database management?
- Database management systems

Why Data Management?

Many computer applications require that data be stored for subsequent processing. Simply storing the data is not enough, however. A computer system can have dozens of disks and tapes, each holding data for dozens of different applications. For any given application, one and only one set of data will do, so the system must be able to store, locate, and retrieve the specific data needed by a given program. That is the concern of **data management**.

Accessing Data

Imagine a single diskette containing several programs. For a particular application, only one of those programs will do. How is a given program selected, loaded, and executed? In Chapter 6 you learned that the operating system, responding to a user's command, reads the disk's directory, searches it for the requested program name, extracts the program's track and sector address, and issues primitive commands to read it into memory. Later, following a RUN command, the program is given control of the processor.

Accessing data presents a similar problem. A single diskette can hold data for several different applications. For a given application, one and only one set of data will do, and finding the right data is much like finding the right program. There are differences between accessing programs and accessing data, however. When a program is needed, all its instructions must be loaded into memory. Data, on the other hand, are typically processed selectively, a few elements at a time. Thus it is not enough merely to locate the data; the system must be able to distinguish among the individual data elements, too.

Data Structures

The key to retrieving data is remembering where they are stored. The basic unit of data, a single fact, is called a **data element**. If the data elements are stored according to a consistent and well-understood **data structure**, it is possible to retrieve them by remembering that structure.

The simplest data structure is a **list**. For example, data for a program that computes an average might be stored as a series of numbers separated by commas (Fig. 8.1). The commas distinguish the data elements. Often, the list is terminated by a sentinel value such as a negative number.

4410, 843, 184, 31, 905, 6357, 44, 7702, 228, 59, −1

Figure 8.1 The simplest data structure is a list.

1,1	1,2	1,3	1,4	1,5
71	38	29	90	70
2,1	2,2	2,3	2,4	2,5
91	13	56	77	20
3,1	3,2	3,3	3,4	3,5
68	18	54	63	56
4,1	4,2	4,3	4,4	4,5
12	38	68	39	74
5,1	5,2	5,3	5,4	5,5
82	80	35	98	61

Figure 8.2 Most programming languages support a more complex data structure called an array.

Most programming languages support a more complex data structure called an **array** (Fig. 8.2). Each array cell or element can hold one data value. Cells are assigned a unique identifying number or numbers, and individual data elements can be inserted, extracted, or manipulated by referencing those numbers. For example, in the array pictured in Fig. 8.2, each cell is identified by a row number and a column number, and row 1, column 3 contains the value 29. Once an array has been filled, it can be written to disk, tape, or any other secondary medium, and later read back into memory for processing.

Suppose you want to write a program to generate name and address labels. For each label you need a name, a street address, a city, a state, and a zip code. A list might do for a few labels, but separating the elements would soon become tedious. An option is to set up an array of names and addresses with each row holding the data for a single label. The only problem is that the entire array must be in memory before the individual elements can be accessed. Main memory space is limited, so even with an array you could generate relatively few labels.

A better solution is to organize the data as a file (Fig. 8.3). All computer data begin as patterns of bits. On a file the bits are grouped to form characters. Groups of characters in turn form meaningful data elements called **fields**. A group of related fields is a **record**; a **file** is a set of related records. For example, in a name and address file, an individual's name is a field. Each record holds a complete set of data for a single individual (a name, a street address, and so on). The file consists of all the records.

Name	Street address	City	State	Zip code
Melinda Atkins	142 Maple St.	Oxford	Ohio	450781718
Charles Baker	713 Main Street	Cincinnati	Ohio	457033304
Thomas Bates	42 South Blvd.	Atlanta	Georgia	352170315
Lisa Campanella	8 Tower Square	San Jose	California	953214450
Shen Chan	State Route 77	Binghamton	New York	127561495
Tomas Garcia	473 Dixie Highway	Lexington	Kentucky	434101236
.	.	.	.	.
.	.	.	.	.
.	.	.	.	.
Arthur White	Northside Mall	Orlando	Florida	214504372

File

Character

Field

Record

Figure 8.3 Characters are grouped to form fields. Fields are grouped to form records. A file is a set of related records.

The data in a file are processed record by record. Normally, the file is stored on a secondary medium such as disk. Programs are written to read a record, process its fields, generate the appropriate output, and then read and process another record. Because only one record is in memory at a time, very little memory is needed. Because many records can be stored on a single disk, a great deal of data can be processed in this limited space.

Locating Files

Imagine a file stored on disk. The first step in accessing its data is finding the file. The task is much like finding a program, but there are differences. Following a command such as LOAD or RUN, programs are loaded by the operating system. Data, on the other hand, are processed by application programs in the context of a program's logic. Typically, just before the data are required, the program asks the operating system to open the file. Each file has a name; the **open** logic (Fig. 8.4) reads the disk directory, searches it by name, and finds the address of the first record in the file.

Locating Records

Once a file has been located, the process of accessing its records can begin. When a program needs input data, it reads a record; when it is ready to output results, it writes a record. Note that these instructions deal with selected records, not with the entire file. Files are opened. Records are read and written.

106

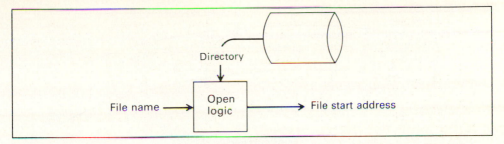

Figure 8.4 When a file is opened, the disk directory is read into memory and searched for the file's name. If the file name is found, the file's start address is extracted from the directory.

A programmer views data logically, requesting the next record or the name and address for a particular customer. The data are stored on a secondary medium such as disk. To access a record physically, the disk drive must be given a set of primitive commands: seeks, reads, and writes. The programmer thinks in terms of **logical I/O**. The external device stores and retrieves physical sectors; it "thinks" in terms of **physical I/O**.

There must be a mechanism for translating the programmer's logical requests to the appropriate physical commands (Fig. 8.5). On small computers, much of the logic is found in the operating system's input/output control system; on larger machines, access methods are used. Increasingly, the programmer's logical data request is translated to physical form by a database management system.

The Relative Record Concept

The key to many data storage and retrieval techniques is the **relative record number**. Imagine a string of 100 records. Number the first one 0, the second 1, the third 2, and so on. The numbers indicate a given record's position relative to the beginning of the file. The file's first record (relative record 0) is at "start of file plus 0;" its second record is at "start of file plus 1," and so on.

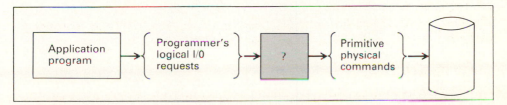

Figure 8.5 Programmers think in terms of logical I/O. A physical device responds to primitive physical commands. In some way, logical I/O requests must be translated to physical commands.

**Data Management
Accessing Data**

107

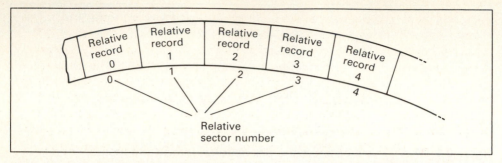

Figure 8.6 A relative number indicates a record's position relative to the first record in a file. Relative sector numbers are generated by counting from the physical file's first sector. Given a relative record number, it is possible to compute a physical disk address.

Now store the records on disk (Fig. 8.6); to keep this example simple, store one per sector. Number the sectors relative to the start of the file: 0, 1, 2, and so on. Note that the relative record number, a logical concept, and the relative sector number, a physical location, are identical. Given a relative record number, it is possible to compute a relative sector number. Given a relative sector number, it is possible to compute a physical disk address.

Assume that a file begins at track 30, sector 0 and that one logical record is stored in each sector. As Fig. 8.7 shows, relative record 0 is stored at track 30,

Relative record number	Actual location on disk	
	Track	Sector
0	30	0
1	30	1
2	30	2
3	30	3
4	30	4
5	30	5
6	30	6
7	30	7
8	30	8
9	30	9
10	30	10
⋮	⋮	⋮

Figure 8.7 Given the start of a file address (from open) and a relative record number, a physical address can be computed.

108

sector 0; relative record 1 is at track 30, sector 1; and so on. Note the pattern. Can you see that relative record 10 must be stored at track 30, sector 10?

In this example the relative record number indicates how many sectors away from the beginning of the file the record is stored. Thus the physical location of any record can be computed by adding its relative record number to the start-of-file address (which, remember, was extracted from the disk's directory when the file was opened). The file starts at track 30, sector 0. Relative record 10 is stored ten sectors away, at track 30, sector 10. To read record 10, the disk drive must be told to seek to track 30 and read sector 10. A logical data request has been translated to specific physical commands.

Some systems address data by relative bytes or characters rather than by relative records. The basic concept, however, is the same. The location of any given data element or group of elements can be computed by counting bytes, words, records, or other units of storage from the beginning of the file.

Other complications are possible, too. For example, you might store two or more logical records in each sector or create a file extending over multiple tracks, but you will still be able to develop a simple algorithm to compute a record's physical location given its relative address. Many different algorithms are used. Some allow records to be stored or retrieved sequentially. Others access records in random order. Data retrieval algorithms are implemented through access methods.

Access Techniques

Sequential Access

Imagine preparing meeting announcements for a club. You need a set of mailing labels, and each member's name and address are recorded on an index card. Probably the easiest way to generate the labels is to copy the data from the first card, turn to the second card and copy it, and so on, processing the records sequentially from the beginning of the file to the end.

Magazine publishers face the same problem with each new issue, but they need labels for tens of thousands of subscribers. Rather than using index cards, they store customer data on disk or magnetic tape, one record per subscriber. The easiest way to ensure that all labels are generated is to process the records in order, proceeding sequentially from the first record in the file to the last one. To simplify handling, the records might be presorted by zip code or mailing zone, but the basic idea of processing the data in physical order still holds.

How does this relate to the relative record concept? A relative record number indicates a record's position on the file. With **sequential access**, processing begins with relative record 0, then moves to relative record 1, then 2, and so on. Accessing data sequentially involves little more than counting. For example, imagine that a program has just finished processing relative record 14. What is the next record? Obviously, relative record 15. You've already seen how a relative record number can be converted to a physical address; it is possible to read and write records in physical order simply by counting them.

Direct Access

Processing records in sequence is not always acceptable. For example, when a subscriber moves, his or her address must be changed. Searching for that subscriber's record sequentially is like looking for a telephone number by reading the phone book line by line. You would not even consider conducting a sequential search for a person's telephone number. Instead, knowing that the names are listed alphabetically, you quickly narrow your search to a portion of a single page and *then* begin reading the entries, ignoring the bulk of the data. The way you use a telephone book is a good example of **direct access**, or **random access**.

A disk drive reads or writes one physical record at a time. To randomly access a record, all the programmer must do is remember its address and ask for it. The problem is remembering all those disk addresses.

One solution is maintaining an **index** of the records. Again, use the name and address file as an example. Imagine that you want to access individual customer records by name. As the file is created, records are written, one at a time, in relative record number order. Additionally, as each record is written, the customer name and the associated relative record number are recorded in an index (Fig. 8.8). After the last record has been written to disk and its position recorded on the index, the index is itself stored.

Key	Relative record
Atkins, Melinda	0
Baker, Charles	1
Bates, Tomas	2
Campanella, Lisa	3
Chan, Shen	4
Garcia, Thomas	5
.	.
.	.
.	.

Figure 8.8 A file index can help when records must be accessed directly.

Once the index has been created, it can be used to find individual records. Assume, for example, that Susan Smith has changed her address. To record her new address on the file, a program could:

1. read the file index,

2. search the index for her name,

3. find her relative record number,

4. compute the disk address and read her record,

5. change her address, and

6. rewrite the record to the same place on disk.

Note that this specific record is accessed directly and that no other records in the file are involved.

The basic idea of direct access is assigning each record an easy-to-remember, logical key and then converting that key to a relative record number. Given this relative location, a physical address can be computed and the record accessed. Using an index is one technique for converting keys to physical addresses. An option is passing a numeric key to an algorithm and computing a relative record number. Both techniques have the same objective: converting a programmer's logical data requests to physical form.

Access Methods

Earlier in the chapter (Fig. 8.5), the gap separating logical and physical I/O was identified. An **access method** is a software module that bridges this gap (Fig. 8.9), converting logical keys to physical addresses and issuing the appropriate primitive commands. There are many variations of sequential, indexed, and direct organizations, and each one has its own access rules. Using a variety of data access techniques can be confusing; this is one reason for the growing popularity of database management systems.

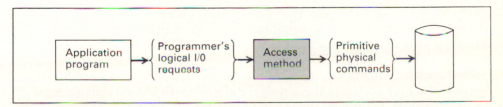

Figure 8.9 Access methods translate a programmer's logical I/O requests to physical commands.

Database Management

Why Database Management?

There are problems with traditional data management. Many of them result from viewing applications independently. For example, consider payroll. Most organizations prepare payroll by computer because using a machine instead of a small army of clerks saves money. Thus the firm develops a payroll program to process a set of payroll files.

Inventory, accounts receivable, accounts payable, and general ledger are similar applications, so the firm develops an inventory program, a set of inventory files, an accounts receivable program, accounts receivable files, and so on. Each program is independent, and each processes its own independent data files.

Why is this a problem? For one thing, different applications often need the same data. For example, schools generate both bills and student grade reports. View the applications independently. The billing program reads a file of billing data, and the grade report program reads an independent file of grade data. The outputs of both programs are mailed to each student's home, so student names and addresses must be redundantly recorded on both files. What happens when a student moves? Unless both files are updated, one will be wrong. **Redundant data** are difficult to maintain.

Data dependency is a more subtle problem. Each access method has its own rules for storing and retrieving data, and certain "tricks of the trade" can significantly improve the efficiency of a given program. Because the motivation for using the computer is saving money, the programmer is often tempted to save even more by taking advantage of these efficiencies. Consequently, the program is written to match the physical structure of the data. When a program's logic is dependent upon its physical data structure, changing that structure will almost certainly require changing the program. As a result, programs using traditional access methods can be difficult to maintain.

The solution to both problems is organizing the data as a single integrated **database**. The task of controlling access to all the data can then be concentrated in a centralized **database management system** (Fig. 8.10).

How does the use of a centralized database solve the data redundancy problem? All data are collected and stored in a single place; consequently, there is one and only one copy of any given data element. When the value of an element (an address, for example) changes, the single database copy is corrected. Any program requiring access to this data element gets the same value because there is only one value.

How does a database help to solve the data dependency problem? Since the responsibility for accessing the physical data rests with the database management system, the programmer can ignore the physical data structure. As a result, programs tend to be much less dependent upon their data and are generally much easier to maintain.

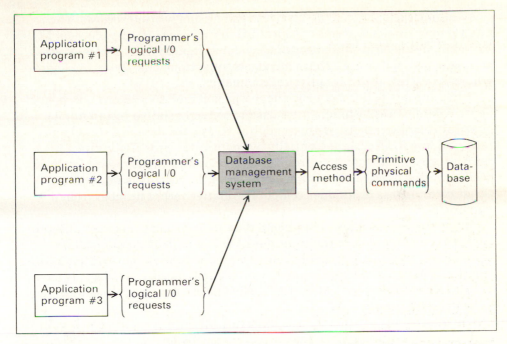

Figure 8.10 A database system insulates the programmer from the physical data.

Database Management Systems

A database management system, or DBMS, is in many ways like a programming language. To create a database, a user specifies the various data structures and their relationships; the DBMS then translates these logical specifications into the necessary physical data structures and links. Once the database is created, the DBMS functions like a super access method, accepting logical I/O requests and originating the physical I/O operations needed to store or retrieve the desired data. A **query language**, a feature of many database management systems, makes it easy for even nontechnical personnel to access the database by essentially asking questions. Query languages are particularly valuable for generating one-time or time-crucial reports.

Summary

In general, the key to retrieving data is using a well defined data structure. The simplest data structure is a list. Most programming languages support a more complex data structure called an array. Many programs access files, with characters grouped to form fields, fields grouped to form records, and records grouped to form a file. A file is located by asking the operating system to open it.

Accessing the data on a file involves reading and writing records. The programmer thinks in terms of logical I/O; hardware performs physical I/O. Software, in the form of the operating system's input/output control system, an access method, or a database management system, translates the logical requests into the necessary physical commands.

Often, the key to finding a specific record is its relative record number. Several data access techniques are used to convert relative record numbers to physical record locations. With sequential access, the data are stored and retrieved in a fixed order, essentially by counting records. With direct or random access, individual records can be retrieved without regard for their position in the physical file. Often, an index of the records is maintained. Other direct access techniques compute a relative record number from a numeric key.

There are problems with traditional data management. Because different applications often require the same data, certain data elements may be stored in several different places, and such redundant data are difficult to maintain. Data dependency is another problem. If a program's logic is too closely linked to the physical structure of its data, that program can be difficult to maintain.

The solution to both problems is collecting all the organization's data in a centralized database. With a database there is only one copy of each data element, so the data redundancy problem is eliminated. Because every program must access data through a database management system, programs are insulated from the physical data structure; thus data dependency is reduced. A database management system includes the logic needed to create, access, and maintain the database. Many also include a query language that allows even nontechnical users to extract data.

Key Words

access method	index
array	list structure
database	logical I/O
database management system	open
data dependency	physical I/O
data element	query language
data management	random access
data structure	record
direct access	redundant data
field	relative record number
file	sequential access

Self-Test

1. The operating system locates a specific program by searching the disk's _____.

2. The simplest data structure is a _____.

3. Data values are accessed by cell or element number (or numbers) in an _____.

4. A single, meaningful data element, such as a person's name, is called a _____.

5. A group of related fields forms a _____.

6. A set of related records forms a _____.

7. The programmer thinks in terms of _____ I/O. A disk drive "thinks" in terms of _____ I/O.

8. Transferring a single sector from disk into main memory is an example of _____ I/O.

9. The _____ is the key to many data storage and retrieval techniques.

10. A programmer's logical I/O requests are converted to physical commands by an _____.

11. Records are processed in the order in which they are stored under _____ processing.

12. With _____ access, records can be accessed in any order.

13. Data _____ occurs when the same data are stored in two or more places.

14. Data _____ occurs when a program's logic is closely tied to a physical data structure.

15. Data redundancy and data dependency can be minimized by using a _____.

Relating the Concepts

1. When a program is accessed, all its instructions are loaded. Data, on the other hand, are accessed selectively. Explain.

2. What is a data structure? Why are data structures important?

3. Relate the terms character, field, record, and file.

4. What happens when a file is opened? Why?

5. Briefly explain the difference between logical I/O and physical I/O.

6. Briefly explain the relative record concept.

7. Distinguish between sequential access and direct access. Relate both access techniques to the relative record concept.

8. What is an access method? Why are access methods needed?

9. What is a database? Why are databases useful?

10. Relate a database management system to an access method. How are they similar? How are they different?

9

Systems Analysis and Design

Preview

Because a computer system consists of numerous components that must work together, creating a new system requires careful planning and coordination. This chapter introduces several basic systems analysis and design principles. Key concepts include:

Systems analysis

- Problem definition
- Analysis
- Requirements specification

Design

Development

Implementation and maintenance

The analyst's methodology

Systems Analysis

A computer-based **system** is a collection of hardware, software, data, people, and procedures that work together to accomplish an objective. Often, the idea for a

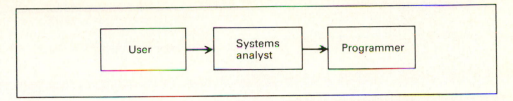

Figure 9.1 A systems analyst translates user needs into technical terms.

system starts with a **user** who needs information. Users generally know what they need but might not have the technical skills to obtain it. Programmers have the expertise but often lack the background to understand the user's problem. A **systems analyst** is a professional who translates user needs into technical specifications (Fig. 9.1).

Perhaps the best way to illustrate what an analyst does is through an example. Imagine that the owner of a clothing store is experiencing an inventory problem. Merchandise is purchased at wholesale, displayed, and sold to customers. Too much stock is an unnecessary expense. On the other hand, a poor selection discourages shoppers. Ideally, a balance can be achieved: enough but not too much.

Unfortunately, inventory is constantly changing, with customer purchases depleting stock and returns and reorders adding to it. The owner would like to be able to track inventory and reorder any given item just before the store runs out. For a single item the task is easy, but the store has hundreds of different items, and keeping track of each one is impractical. The owner recently saw an advertisement for a computer-based inventory system. It looked interesting, but none of the store personnel knows anything about computers. Thus a systems analyst has been asked to look into the problem.

Problem Definition

Often, the analyst starts with little more than a vague sense of the problem; in this example the owner is not satisfied with inventory and feels that a computer might help. The first step in the **systems analysis** process is to develop a more precise **problem definition**. The objective is to determine what the user needs.

At this stage, although the user might not be able to state the problem clearly, he or she knows more about what is needed than the analyst does, so the analyst's job is to observe, listen, and learn. After a period of observation, interviews, and careful study, a formal problem definition is written and submitted to the user for approval. The time to catch misunderstandings and oversights is now—before time, money, and effort are wasted.

Often, following a preliminary problem definition, the analyst performs a **feasibility study** to determine whether the problem can be solved and whether it is worth solving. If the answer is no, the system should not be developed.

Systems Analysis and Design
Systems Analysis

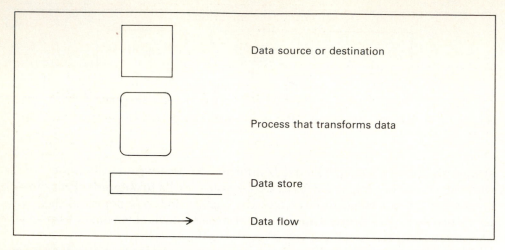

Figure 9.2 A data flow diagram uses four symbols to represent the components of a logical system.

Analysis

As **analysis** begins, the analyst understands the problem and believes that it can and should be solved. The next step is to determine *what* must be done to solve it. The objective is to develop a **logical system** design; at this stage, no physical components are specified. Often, the first step is to identify the system's basic functions. For example, stock levels change because customers purchase, exchange, and return products, so the system will have to process customer transactions.

Data flow diagrams are a particularly useful tool for gaining a sense of the logical relationships between functions. Four symbols are used (Fig. 9.2). Input data enter the system from a source, and output data flow to a destination. Once in the system, the data are manipulated by processes; a process might be a program, a procedure, or anything else that changes or moves data. Data can be held for later processing in a data store, which might be a disk file, a tape file, a database, written notes, or even a person's memory. Data move between sources, destinations, processes, and data stores over data flows.

Figure 9.3 shows a high-level data flow diagram for the inventory system. Transactions flow from a CUSTOMER into the system, where they are handled by *Process transaction*. A data store, STOCK, holds data on each item in inventory; *Process transaction* changes stock levels in response to transactions. MANAGEMENT accesses the system through *Communicate*, evaluating the data in STOCK and, if necessary, requesting a reorder. Once a reorder is authorized, *Generate reorder* sends necessary data to the SUPPLIER, who ships the items to the store.

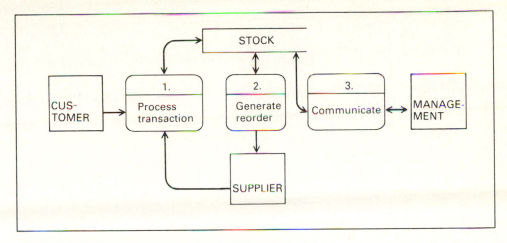

Figure 9.3 A data flow diagram of the inventory system.

To check the data flow diagram, the analyst traces the data flows. Start with destination SUPPLIER. Reorders flow to suppliers; for example, the store might want 25 pairs of jeans. To fill the order, the supplier needs the product description and the reorder quantity. The product description and the reorder quantity are output by *Generate reorder*. Data flow into *Generate reorder* from STOCK, so product descriptions and reorder quantities must be in STOCK.

The process of checking data flows helps to verify the data flow diagram. To keep track of the data elements, they are listed in a **data dictionary** (Fig. 9.4), a collection of data that describes and defines the data. A simple data dictionary can be set up on index cards, but computerized versions are much more efficient.

Each process in the data flow diagram represents an **algorithm**. At this stage, algorithms are defined by listing their inputs and outputs and briefly describing necessary operations. Later, during design, considerably more detail is added.

Data flow diagrams, data dictionaries, and algorithm descriptions provide a format for recording information about the proposed system. These three tools are related. Every process must have an algorithm description. Every algorithm must have a matching process in the data flow diagram. Every element in the data dictionary must appear in at least one data flow. Every element moving through the data flow diagram must be listed in the data dictionary. Cross-referencing these three tools highlights oversights and missing pieces. This verification process is tedious, but modern computer-aided software engineering (CASE) tools can help.

The data flow diagram, the data dictionary, and the algorithm descriptions document the analyst's understanding of the system requirements. By reviewing these documents the user can correct misunderstandings and

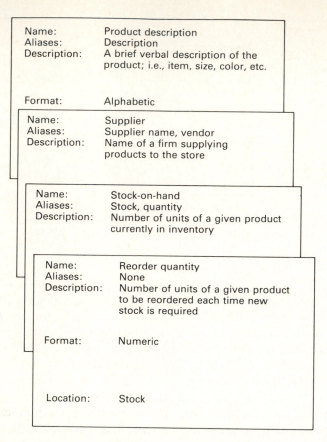

Figure 9.4 Data elements are formally documented in a data dictionary.

errors; after all, the point of the system is to meet the user's needs. Note that no *physical* components have been defined. During analysis the systems analyst designs a *logical* system.

Requirements Specification

On large projects the analyst might prepare a formal, detailed **requirements specification** to document the logical system. These specifications can be hundreds of pages long and are common in competitive bidding situations.

Design

As **design** begins, the analyst knows what the system must do and thus can begin planning *how* to do it. During design, the programs, procedures, files, and other components that comprise the **physical system** are identified and defined.

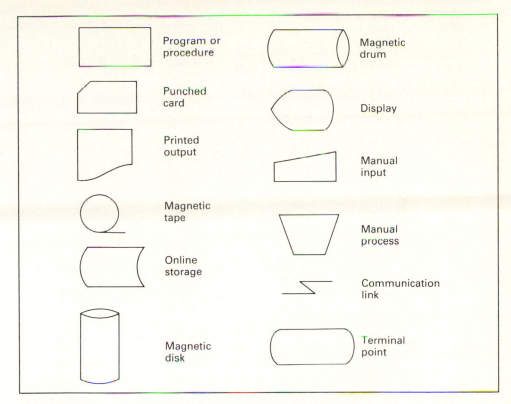

Figure 9.5 On a system flowchart, symbols represent programs, procedures, hardware devices, and the other components of a physical system.

The data flow diagram lists the necessary functions. How might they be implemented? One possibility is writing one program for each process. Another is combining two or more processes in a single program. There are numerous alternative solutions, and a good analyst will investigate several of them.

A **system flowchart** uses symbols to represent programs, procedures, hardware devices, and the other components of a physical system (Fig. 9.5). For example, the flowchart pictured in Fig. 9.6 illustrates one possible high-level design for the inventory system. It shows that transaction data enter through a terminal. Once in the system, they are processed by a program and then stored on an inventory file. The file is processed by a second program through which management manipulates the data and authorizes reorders.

The system flowchart maps the system, highlighting its major physical parts. Key hardware components include a computer, a disk drive, a data entry terminal, a printer, and a display terminal. Two programs are needed: *Process transaction* and *Report and reorder*. Since the data link the components, the next task is defining the data structures; for example, the inven-

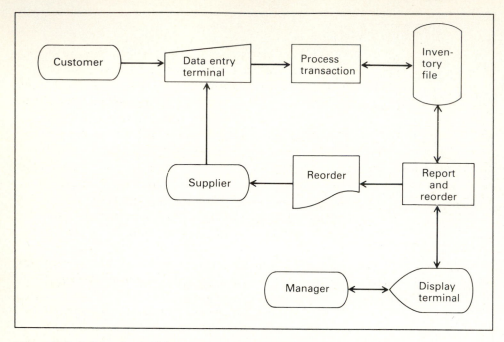

Figure 9.6 A flowchart of the proposed physical system.

tory file contains all the data elements from data store STOCK. The data dictionary is the primary reference for defining the data structures.

How should the inventory file be organized? In some applications, data are collected over time and are processed together as a batch. If **batch processing** is acceptable, a sequential file is probably best. It is not always possible to wait until a batch of transactions is collected, however. For example, in an air defense system, if an unidentified aircraft is spotted, it must be identified immediately; the idea of waiting until 5:00 P.M. because "that's when the air defense program is run" is absurd. On such systems, each transaction must be processed as it occurs. Generally, **transaction processing** calls for direct access files. The key to selecting a file organization is defining the timing requirements of each of the programs.

During analysis a sketchy description of the algorithms was adequate, but the programmer will need considerably more detail. Writing precise algorithm descriptions is another important design task.

Often, the analyst will develop several alternative system designs and perform a cost/benefit analysis for each one. The final selection is made by the user or by management. Once a design is agreed upon, the data structures, file organizations, algorithm descriptions, and system flowchart become a blueprint for the system.

Development

Programs are defined in the context of a system. Given the necessary data structures and algorithms, a programmer can begin to plan the program's logic. Several planning tools might be used. Flowcharts graphically represent a program's logic. With pseudocode the programmer can "draft" the logic before converting it to source code. More complex programs might be written by teams of programmers. Such programs are typically broken into relatively small, single-function modules that can be independently coded; hierarchy charts can be used to show how the modules are linked. Much as a contractor prepares detailed blueprints before starting to build a house, a programmer develops a detailed plan before starting to write code.

During the **coding** stage the programmer translates the plan into source statements. Once the program is coded, it must be **debugged**. The compiler or interpreter usually spots mechanical errors such as incorrect punctuation or spelling; but finding and correcting logical errors, or bugs, that result from coding the wrong instructions is much more difficult. Careful planning is crucial because it simplifies program debugging.

Program **documentation** consists of diagrams, comments, and other descriptive materials that explain or clarify the code. Documentation is invaluable during program debug and essential for efficient program maintenance.

Other tasks are performed during development, too. Files are created and their contents verified. New hardware is purchased, installed, and tested. Operating procedures and training materials are written, and a test plan is developed. Forms and other documents are designed. This phase of the analyst's job requires considerable attention to detail.

Implementation and Maintenance

When all the components are ready, the system is tested. Frequently, bugs and misunderstandings are unearthed even at this late date, and they must be corrected. Eventually, the user is satisfied, and the system is released. Often, training user personnel is a crucial part of the **implementation** phase.

Maintenance begins after the system is released. As people use the system, they suggest improvements and enhancements. Occasionally, undetected bugs appear and must be removed. More generally, conditions change, and the system must be updated. For example, if the government passes a law changing the procedure for collecting income taxes, the payroll program must be modified. Maintenance continues for the life of the system, and its cost can easily match or exceed the original development cost. Good planning and documentation can help to minimize maintenance cost.

The Analyst's Methodology

Note that the analyst moves from the original problem definition to the final system implementation by following a careful, methodical, step-by-step process. The problem is defined before analysis begins. The logical system is specified before design begins. Design is completed before the programmers begin writing code. The system is tested before it is released. This methodology helps to ensure that nothing is overlooked.

Note also how the level of technical detail increases from step to step. Initially, the analyst works with the user. Next, user needs are restated in broad, conceptual, logical terms. Finally, detailed program, file, and hardware specifications, test plans, and operating procedures are written. A professional systems analyst must be able to work with the "big picture" *and* the technical details. Good analysts are hard to find.

Summary

A system is a collection of hardware, software, data, and procedural components that work together to accomplish an objective. Systems are planned and designed by systems analysts. The first step in the process is problem definition. Often, a feasibility study is conducted to determine whether the problem can be solved.

During analysis the analyst develops a logical model of the system. Key tools include data flow diagrams, a data dictionary, and algorithm descriptions. Detailed requirements specifications are prepared for some large systems.

The analyst defines the physical system during the design phase. A system flowchart maps the system's components. Data structures and precise algorithm descriptions are prepared. Ideally, the analyst considers several alternative solutions before settling on one.

During the development stage, programs are planned and written, hardware is ordered and installed, procedures are developed, and files and databases are initialized. Finally, during implementation the pieces are assembled and tested. Following release of the system, maintenance begins.

An analyst uses a precise methodology to move from design to implementation. A good analyst can work with broad concepts and technical details.

Key Words

algorithm

analysis

batch processing

coding

data dictionary

data flow diagram

debug

design

documentation

feasibility study

implementation

logical system

maintenance

physical system

problem definition

requirements specification

system

system flowchart

systems analysis

systems analyst

transaction processing

user

Self-Test

1. A _____ is a collection of components that work together to accomplish an objective.

2. A _____ is a professional who translates user needs into technical terms.

3. The first step in the systems analysis and design process is _____.

4. During problem definition the _____ is the analyst's primary source of information.

5. A systems analyst might conduct a _____ to determine whether a problem can be solved.

6. During analysis the analyst plans a _____ system.

7. A logical system design is documented by _____, _____, and _____.

8. Concern for the physical structure of the system begins during _____.

9. A physical system design can be mapped by drawing a _____.

10. A _____ file organization is probably best for a batch processing application.

11. A _____ file organization is probably best for a transaction processing application.

12. Errors are removed from a program during _____.

13. Program _____ consists of comments and other materials that explain or describe the logic.

14. A system is released as part of the _____ process.

15. After a system is "finished," _____ begins.

Relating the Concepts

1. What is a system?

2. Programs are defined and planned in the context of a system. Explain.

3. What does a systems analyst do? Why is someone like a systems analyst needed?

4. List the steps in the systems analysis and design process, and briefly explain what happens during each step.

5. During problem definition the analyst must communicate with the user in the user's own terms. Why?

6. What is a feasibility study?

7. Briefly explain the difference between a logical system and a physical system.

8. A systems analyst follows a methodical, step-by-step process when developing a system. Why?

9. Distinguish between batch processing and transaction processing.

10. A good systems analyst will consider several alternative physical system designs before selecting one. Why?

Multiple-User Systems

Preview

To take advantage of the power of a large computer system, it is necessary to allow numerous users to share its resources. Sharing leads to conflicts, and those conflicts are resolved by the operating system. This chapter describes the functions performed by a multiple-user operating system. Key concepts include:

Multiprogramming

Multiprogramming operating systems

- Managing the processor's time
- Memory management
- Peripheral device allocation
- Scheduling
- Spooling

Time-sharing

Multiprocessing

Multiprogramming

Early computers were capable of executing a few thousand instructions per second. Modern mainframes are much faster, executing millions of instructions per second. Unfortunately, peripheral devices have not kept pace. Keyboards are driven by human beings—how fast can you type? Card readers, printers, and similar devices transmit, at best, a few thousand characters per second, and even "high-speed" secondary storage is a poor match for a computer. A modern mainframe is capable of processing data thousands of times faster than its peripheral devices can supply them.

What does the computer do during input or output? Nothing. A program cannot process data it does not yet have, and the success of an output operation cannot be assumed until the operation is finished, so the program waits. Since the program controls the computer, the computer waits, too.

Because it is so much faster than its peripherals, a computer typically spends far more time waiting for input and output than it does processing data. During a single second a large mainframe can execute a million instructions or more, so each unused second represents a tremendous waste of potential computing power. The problem is a bit like running a high-speed train on poorly maintained tracks. What good is speed you can't use?

Why not put two programs in memory? Then, when program A is waiting for data, the processor can turn its attention to program B (Fig. 10.1). And why stop at two programs? With three programs, even more otherwise wasted time is utilized (Fig. 10.2). Generally, the more programs in memory, the greater the utilization of the processor. This technique is called **multiprogramming**.

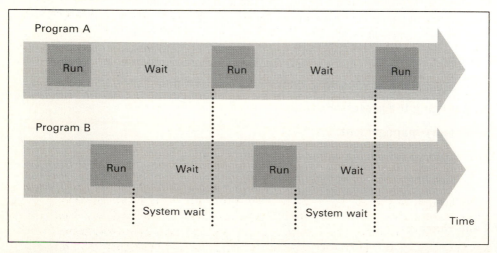

Figure 10.1 With two programs in memory, the processor can switch its attention to program B when program A is waiting for input or output.

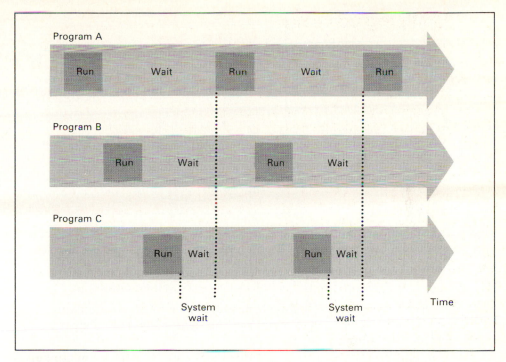

Figure 10.2 More programs in memory means that even more "wait" time can be utilized.

Note that although several programs are in memory, the processor still fetches and executes a single instruction during each machine cycle. If the processor can execute only one *instruction* at a time, it cannot possibly work on more than one *program* at a time. Simultaneous means "at the same instant." No one can study and watch television simultaneously. No processor can execute two or more programs simultaneously. **Concurrent** means "over the same time period." Some students can concurrently study and watch television. A processor can certainly execute two or more programs concurrently.

Multiprogramming Operating Systems

The advantages of multiprogramming are obvious: more programs can be run in the same amount of time on the same computer. However, while a computer's resources are substantial, they are limited, so when two or more concurrent users share a computer, conflicts over processor time, memory space, and peripheral device allocations are inevitable. When these conflicts occur, they must be resolved. Since human operators cannot function at computer speeds, key decisions must be made by the computer itself.

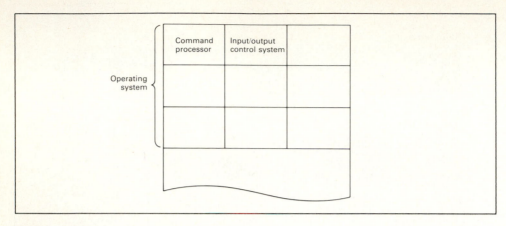

Figure 10.3 Most elementary operating systems contain a command processor and an input/output control system. Multiprogramming operating systems are built on this base.

Because a computer's **operating system** serves as a hardware/software interface, its "in-between" position makes it an ideal place to implement **resource management**.

You first encountered operating systems in Chapter 6, where you studied two modules: the command processor and the input/output control system (Fig. 10.3). Because a mainframe is composed of so many components, its command processor and IOCS are more complex than a microcomputer's, but the functions performed are similar. A multiprogramming operating system builds on this base, adding modules to manage processor time, main memory space, and peripheral devices.

Managing the Processor's Time

Start with **processor management**. Imagine that two programs, A and B, are in memory. Some time ago, program A requested data from disk (Fig. 10.4). The input operation was assigned to a channel, and the processor

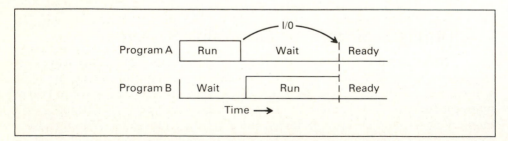

Figure 10.4 With multiple concurrent users, it is possible that two or more programs will be ready to execute at the same time. When this happens, an operating system module must resolve the conflict, deciding which program goes first.

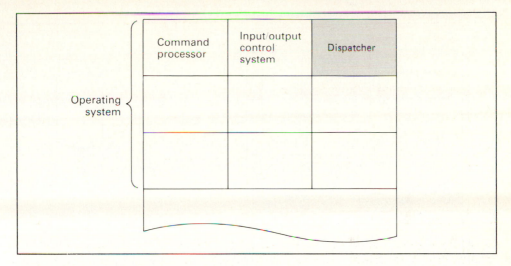

Figure 10.5 The processor's time is managed by the dispatcher.

turned to program B. Assume that the input operation has just been completed. *Both* programs are ready to run. Which one gets the processor?

One possible solution is to display a message on the console asking the operator to make a decision. The operator will need at least a second or two to respond. During that brief time the processor can easily execute instructions for *both* programs. Computers are so fast that a human being cannot effectively make such real-time choices. On most multiprogramming systems the processor's time is managed by an operating system module called the **dispatcher** (Fig. 10.5).

How does the dispatcher know when to switch from one program to another? The key is I/O. A program loses control of the processor when it starts an input or output operation and is eligible to regain control when that operation is complete. If the dispatcher is to decide which program goes next, it must know when input or output operations begin and end. Electronic signals called **interrupts** are used to mark these events. When an interrupt is sensed, no matter what the computer might be doing, hardware automatically transfers control to an operating system module that deals with the interrupt and then calls the dispatcher.

Follow the steps in Fig. 10.6. When an application program needs data, it issues an interrupt (Fig. 10.6a). In response, hardware transfers control to the operating system. Once it gets control, the operating system drops the application program into a **wait state** (Fig. 10.6b), starts the input or output operation, and then calls the dispatcher, which starts another application program (Fig. 10.6c). Later, when the I/O operation is finished, the *channel* issues an interrupt (Fig. 10.6d). Once again the operating system gets control (Fig. 10.6e) and marks the program needing data as "ready." Then it calls the dispatcher, which starts an application program (Fig. 10.6f).

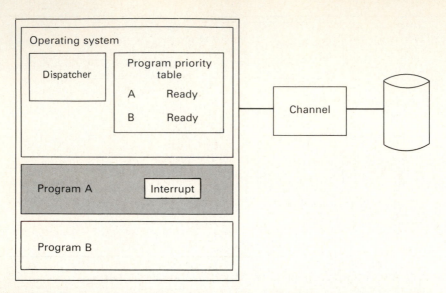

Figure 10.6 The key to managing the processor's time is recognizing when input and output operations begin and end. Generally, these crucial events are signaled by interrupts. **(a)** When an application program needs data, it issues an interrupt.

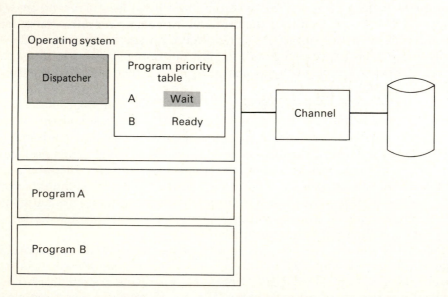

Figure 10.6(b) Following the interrupt, the operating system gets control and sets the program to a wait state.

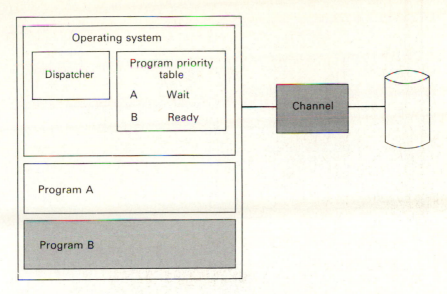

Figure 10.6(c) After the requested input or output operation is started, the dispatcher gives control to another application program.

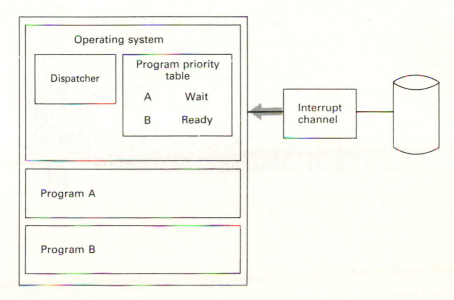

Figure 10.6(d) Eventually, the channel signals the end of the I/O operation by sending the computer an interrupt.

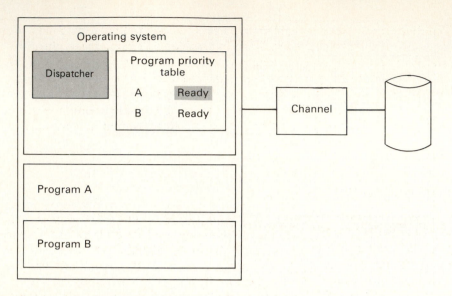

Figure 10.6(e) Following the interrupt, the operating system gets control and resets program A to a ready state.

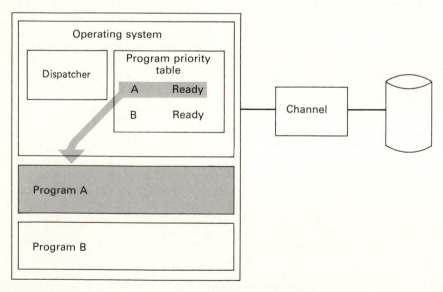

Figure 10.6(f) Finally, the dispatcher selects the next application program.

The dispatcher uses an algorithm to decide which program goes next. For example, if all the programs are listed in a table in priority order, the dispatcher can scan this table after each interrupt and select the first "ready" program it encounters. Priority rules might be based on such criteria as a program's size, location in memory, time in memory, or the significance of the information it produces. The key point is that once the algorithm has been set up, the priority decision is handled by the operating system at computer speed.

Memory Management

Memory management is concerned with allocating memory space to application programs; like processor management, it is the responsibility of the operating system (Fig 10.7). The simplest approach, **fixed partition memory management** (Fig. 10.8), divides the available space into fixed-length partitions and stores one program in each. More efficient memory utilization is achieved with **dynamic memory management**. Using this technique, the available memory is treated as a large pool of free space, and each program is assigned exactly as much as it needs.

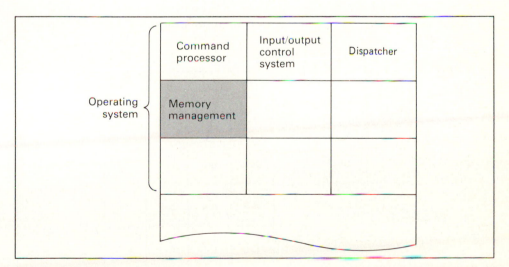

Figure 10.7 Memory management is another operating system responsibility.

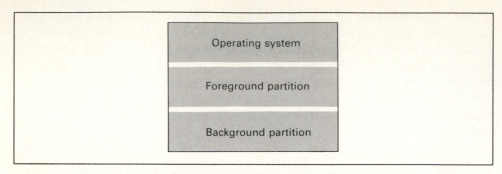

Figure 10.8 Under fixed partition memory management, the available memory is divided into fixed-length partitions.

If a computer can execute only one instruction at a time, why must an entire program be loaded into memory? Why not load only the active parts? On **virtual memory** systems, application programs are placed in secondary storage, and portions are moved into memory as needed (Fig. 10.9). These "partial" programs require less space than would complete programs. Since less space is needed for each program, more programs can be loaded into the same amount of memory. More programs means more efficient processor utilization.

Peripheral Device Allocation

What would happen if two programs were to take turns writing to the same printer? The output would be useless. Or imagine programs A and B taking

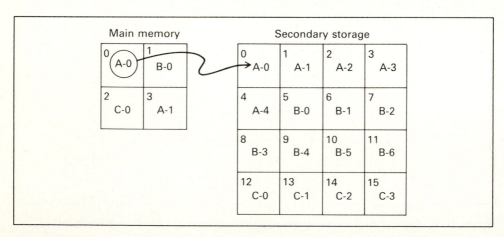

Figure 10.9 On a virtual memory system, portions of programs move back and forth between main memory and secondary storage. **(a)** An unneeded portion of a program is copied to secondary storage.

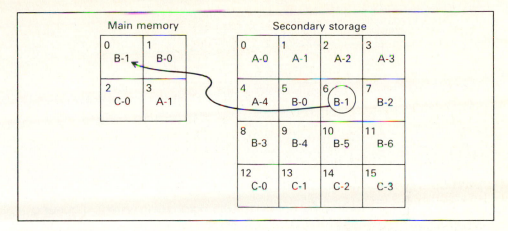

Figure 10.9(b) A needed portion of another program replaces it in memory.

turns writing and reading data to and from the same tape. The result would be chaos! This cannot be allowed to happen; access to I/O devices must be carefully managed. The operating system is responsible for **peripheral device allocation** (Fig. 10.10).

Scheduling

Processor management is concerned with the internal priorities of programs that are already in memory. As a program finishes processing and space becomes available, which program is loaded into memory next? This decision typically involves two separate modules, a job **queuing** routine and a **scheduler** (Fig. 10.10).

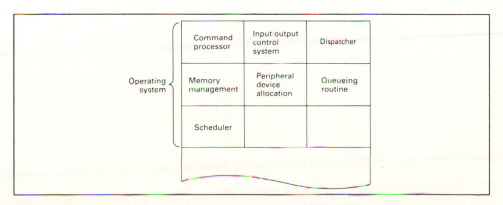

Figure 10.10 The operating system also allocates input, output, and secondary storage devices, enques programs, schedules programs for loading into memory, and performs a number of other support functions.

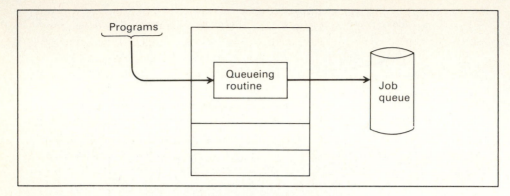

Figure 10.11 When a program first enters a multiprogramming system, a queuing routine copies it to a queue on a secondary storage device.

As programs enter the system, they are placed on a queue by the job queuing routine (Fig. 10.11). When space becomes available, the scheduler selects a program from the queue and loads it into memory (Fig. 10.12). Often, the first program on the queue is the first one loaded, but more sophisticated priority rules can be used. Once a program is in memory, the scheduler is no longer concerned with it. Instead, that program's right to access the processor is determined by the dispatcher.

Spooling

The value of multiprogramming is that more programs can be run in the same amount of time. If the turnover rate of those programs can be increased,

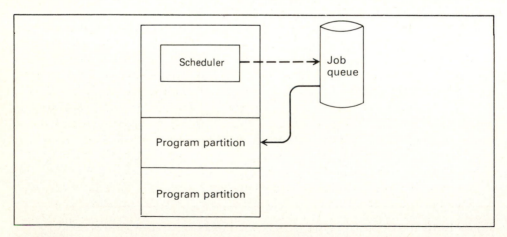

Figure 10.12 Later, when space becomes available, the scheduler loads a program from the queue into memory.

even greater efficiencies can be realized. For example, imagine that a given system executes five concurrent programs and that each program occupies memory for ten seconds. As soon as a program finishes executing, another one replaces it in memory, so the computer can run thirty programs a minute. If each program's run time could be reduced to five seconds, 60 programs could run in that same minute.

Picture a program that generates payroll for 1000 employees. Reading 1000 time cards takes at least two minutes. Printing 1000 checks takes a few minutes more, so the program will need at least four or five minutes to run. But what if the slow card reader and printer were replaced by a disk? A disk drive is much faster, so the program would run in much less time. Consequently, memory would be freed for another program much more quickly.

That's the essential idea behind **spooling**. Even with multiprogramming, it's common for all application programs to be waiting for I/O. When this happens, the processor has nothing to do. During these idle periods the operating system's spooling module reads data from such slow devices as card readers or terminals and stores them on a high-speed medium such as disk, even before the program needing those data has been loaded into memory. Later, when the program is loaded, its input data can be read from disk. On output, data are spooled to disk and later dumped to the printer. Because the application program deals only with high-speed I/O, it finishes processing much more quickly, thus freeing space for another program.

Time-Sharing

Perhaps you have used a terminal to write original programs, execute existing software, or access data. Almost certainly, your terminal, along with dozens, even hundreds of others, was linked to a central computer. Such configurations often involve **time-sharing**.

Imagine a typical time-sharing application. Transactions—single program statements, lines of input data, or commands—are typed through a keyboard. In most cases, very little actual processing is required. Typing is slow; two transactions per minute is the best most people can do. To the computer, each user represents a string of brief, widely spaced processing demands.

As a transaction is processed, the system knows that considerable time will pass before that user's next transaction is received, so once the transaction is processed, the work space can be copied to secondary storage, making room for another application in memory. Later, when the first user's next transaction arrives, his or her work space is read back into memory.

Imagine that you have just spent 20 minutes typing the data for a statistical analysis program. Each data element was one brief transaction; your work to this point certainly fits the pattern of a typical time-shared job. Your last transaction, however, is different. It's a command that tells the system to process the data, and it requests execution of a computational routine that can easily run for two or three minutes. While your transaction is being processed, every other user will have to wait, and that is intolerable.

The solution is to restrict each program to a maximum "slice" of time, perhaps 0.01 second. If, during this interval, processing is completed, fine; control shifts to another program. If not, however, the long-running program is interrupted and moved to the end of the queue to await another turn.

Multiprocessing

Multiprogramming and time-sharing require a resident operating system to deal with the conflicts that arise when multiple concurrent users share limited resources. Both techniques help to improve the efficiency of a system, allowing more programs to be processed in the same time on the same hardware. However, the operating system modules, essential though they may be, occupy memory and consume processor time; they represent unproductive overhead.

Consider, for example, the problem of controlling I/O. Channels were developed to relieve the processor of much of this responsibility. Unfortunately, a channel can't do the whole job itself; certain logical functions such as starting, finishing, and checking the status of the I/O operation were, until recently, performed by the main processor working under the control of the operating system.

Why not identify the operating system code that performs these functions and program a microprocessor to do the same things? Replace the channel with this new I/O processor (Fig. 10.13). Now, because there are two inde-

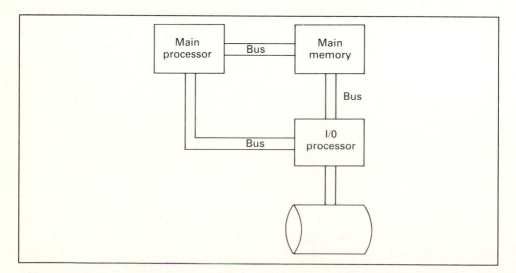

Figure 10.13 If a channel is replaced by an I/O processor, the main processor can be relieved of all responsibility for controlling I/O operations.

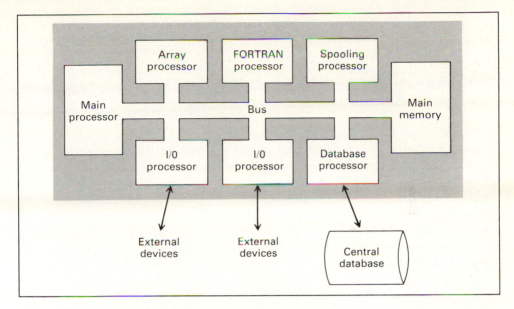

Figure 10.14 In the near future, many overhead functions will be assigned to independent processors, thus freeing the main processor to work on application programs.

pendent processors, the instructions associated with I/O can be executed in parallel with more productive main processor activities. Two processors share the same memory, forming a **multiprocessing** system.

If I/O control can be shifted to an independent processor, why not other functions (Fig. 10.14)? Near-future systems might contain several I/O processors, one to replace each channel. A database processor incorporating much of the logic of a database management system might control all communications with the database. For large scientific and engineering problems an array processor might relieve the main processor of the time-consuming chore of array manipulation. Language processors might allow the direct execution of programs written in a high-level language, thus bypassing the inefficient compilation step. If many of the functions now associated with operating systems and system software are shifted to independent processors, these control programs (overhead) will no longer tie up the main processor's time. The result will be greater efficiency.

Summary

A mainframe computer is much faster than its peripheral devices and thus spends more time waiting for I/O than processing data. With multi-programming, two or more programs are loaded into memory, and the processor executes them concurrently. With multiple programs competing for the computer's limited resources, conflicts are inevitable. Most are resolved by the operating system.

The operating system manages the processor's time. The beginning and end of each input and output operation is marked by an interrupt. After each interrupt, the dispatcher selects the next program by following a priority algorithm.

The simplest form of memory management divides memory into fixed-length partitions. Greater efficiency can be achieved by using dynamic memory management. With virtual memory management, programs are stored on disk, and only active portions are loaded into memory. Another operating system module allocates peripheral devices to application programs.

When programs enter a multiprogrammed system, they are stored on a queue. Later, when memory space becomes available, a scheduler selects the next program from the queue and loads it. Spooling improves the turnover rate of programs.

Time-sharing is often used when numerous terminals must access a system. Under multiprocessing, two or more independent processors share a common memory. Multiprocessing can greatly reduce the processor time lost to nonproductive overhead functions.

Key Words

concurrent	peripheral device allocation
dispatcher	processor management
dynamic memory management	queuing
fixed partition memory management	resource management
interrupt	scheduler
memory management	spooling
multiprocessing	time-sharing
multiprogramming	virtual memory
operating system	wait state

Self-Test

1. A typical mainframe computer spends most of its time _____ rather than processing data.

2. With _____, two or more programs are loaded into memory and executed concurrently.

3. The word _____ means "over the same time period."

4. A computer's resources are managed by its _____.

5. The processor's time is managed by the _____.

6. An operating system can switch from program to program by responding to _____.

7. A program waiting for the completion of an input or output operation is said to be in a _____ state.

8. Under _____ memory management, memory space is divided into fixed-length partitions.

9. Under _____ memory management, each program is allocated as much space as it needs.

10. With _____ memory management, programs are stored on disk, and only active portions are loaded into memory.

11. As programs enter a multiprogramming system, they are stored on a _____.

12. Programs are loaded into memory by the operating system's _____.

13. _____ involves copying data from a slow-speed device to a high-speed device for eventual input to a program.

14. A system with a hundred or more terminals serviced by a central computer is probably a _____ system.

15. With _____, two or more independent processors share the same memory.

Relating the Concepts

1. Imagine that a computer's memory contains only a single program. During input and output the processor can do nothing. Why?

2. Briefly explain multiprogramming.

3. Distinguish the terms "simultaneous" and "concurrent."

4. Why is the operating system such a good place to implement resource management?

5. What is an interrupt? Why are interrupts important to processor management on a multiprogrammed system?

6. On a virtual memory system, most of a given program is stored on a secondary device, and only active portions are actually loaded into memory. Why?

7. Distinguish between scheduling and spooling.

8. Processor management is concerned with the priority of programs that are already in memory, while scheduling and queuing are concerned with the priorities of programs that are not yet in memory. Explain the difference.

9. Briefly explain time sharing. How is memory space managed on a time-shared system? How is processor time managed?

10. Distinguish between multiprogramming and multiprocessing.

11

Data Communication and Networks

Preview

Because a computer's users are often geographically dispersed, it is often necessary to allow them to access the computer over communication lines. This chapter introduces some basic data communication and network principles. Key concepts include:

Networks

- Network configurations

Signals

- Modulation and demodulation

- Analog and digital transmission

Communication systems

- Communication media

- Protocols

- Network management

- Data communication software

Networks

Historically, computers were so expensive that most large organizations did all their data processing on a single, centralized machine. While quite efficient for such tasks as generating payroll and accounting reports, the centralized approach could not effectively provide a quick response to a unique, local problem. Centralized data processing is inconvenient because the people who need information do not necessarily work in the computer center.

During the 1970s, many organizations began to support remote access by linking **terminals** to their mainframes. A terminal is an input/output device that consists of a keyboard, a display screen, and (sometimes) a printer. Terminals allow remote users to access a computer and perform such tasks as data entry, data retrieval, and report generation. A terminal operates under the control of the central computer, responding to commands issued by that central computer.

Given today's low-cost computers, almost anyone who wants one can have one, but multiple stand-alone machines are difficult to maintain and support. The solution is often to link them. Two or more computers linked by communication lines form a **network** (Fig. 11.1). The computers that compose the

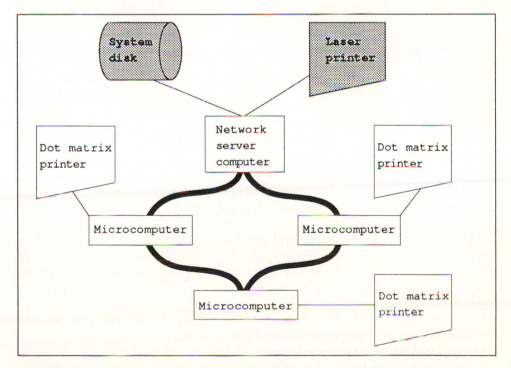

Figure 11.1   A network consists of two or more computers linked by communication lines.

network can share data, hardware resources, and software and, because they are still *computers*, can be used independently to solve local problems.

Many networks support a central database. Users working through remote computers can access the database via the network. With this central source of data it is easy to provide up-to-date information to all users.

Resource sharing is another advantage. For example, a laser printer produces higher-quality output than a dot matrix printer, but at a significantly higher cost. Attaching a laser printer to each user's microcomputer is much too expensive for most organizations. But with a network, users can generate draft-quality output on their own inexpensive dot matrix printers and send finished documents over the network to a shared laser printer.

In many organizations, software sharing was the most important reason for implementing a network. Popular commercial packages, such as dBASE III Plus, WordPerfect 5.0, and Lotus 1-2-3, are sold under a license agreement that, essentially, limits use to one machine per copy. Consequently, the organization faced the almost impossible task of stocking, distributing, maintaining, and accounting for dozens, sometimes even hundreds, of individual program disks.

Given a network, a single copy of each program can be stored on the central database. Then, on demand, the program can be downloaded to a user's computer. With only one copy, software maintenance is greatly simplified. Because all access is through the central computer, appropriate accounting records are easily maintained. Recognizing the value of this approach, most software development firms offer special network versions of their programs.

Network Configurations

Figure 11.1 shows a typical microcomputer network configuration. One computer, the **network server**, controls the network. It houses the central database and other shared resources. The user computers are linked to the network server by wires; often, a single loop runs from the server through each user computer, and then back to the server. *All* communication is routed through the network server.

One alternative is to link the network's computers to form a hierarchy (Fig. 11.2). For example, in a supermarket checkout system, several checkout station microcomputers are linked to the store's minicomputer, and the store minis, in turn, are linked to a central mainframe at supermarket headquarters. A *ring* network (Fig. 11.3) allows an organization's divisions and offices to exchange information. Less obvious is the backup provided by such a network; if one computer fails, its work can be switched to the others.

On a **local area network**, all the computers are in a limited area, typically within a single building or on a single campus. Often, dedicated wires are used, but some local area networks use existing internal telephone wires

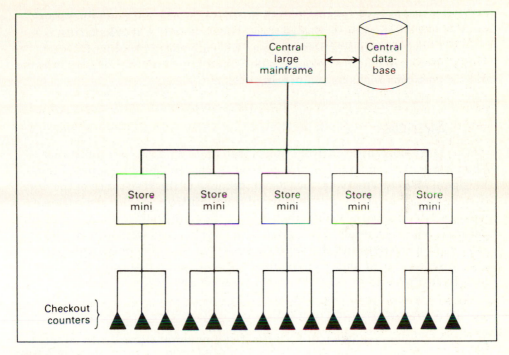

Figure 11.2   A hierarchical network.

to carry both voice and data. **A wide area network** is composed of computers that are more widely separated. In most cases, at least some data are
transmitted over public or leased telephone lines or by other communication
services.

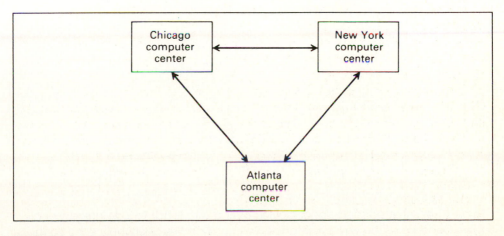

Figure 11.3   A ring network.

Local area networks generally link microcomputers, with one microcomputer or a minicomputer acting as the network server. A **workstation** is a powerful microcomputer, often equipped with advanced graphics features. Workstations are usually linked to a dedicated minicomputer or a mainframe and support such tasks as engineering design.

Signals

Data communication implies transmitting data over a distance. When a signal is transmitted over a distance, several things happen. First, the signal loses intensity or "dies down" because of the resistance of the wire (Fig. 11.4); this problem is called **signal degradation**. At the same time it picks up interference or **noise**; the static in the background of a distant radio station is a good example. The signal grows weaker and weaker as it moves away from its source, and the noise becomes more intense until eventually the signal is overwhelmed. If data are to be sent over a distance, the noise must be filtered and the signal boosted occasionally.

Modulation and Demodulation

Data are often transmitted in the context of a **carrier signal** such as the sine wave pictured in Fig. 11.5. One complete "S-on-its-side" pattern is called a cycle. The height of the wave is its amplitude; the number of cycles per second is its frequency. Because the carrier signal's frequency and amplitude are known, equipment can be designed to filter and boost it.

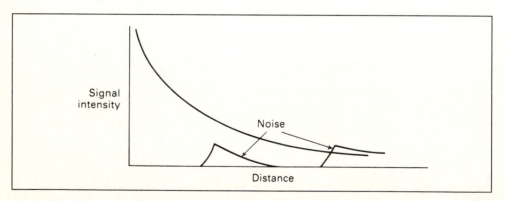

Figure 11.4 An electronic signal moving over a wire tends to lose intensity or die down because of the wire's resistance. Eventually, noise overwhelms the signal, and no data can be transmitted.

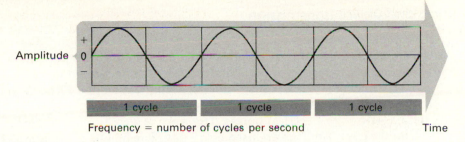

Amplitude

Frequency = number of cycles per second   Time

Figure 11.5   Often, data are carried in the context of a carrier signal such as this sine wave.

A data signal is merged with the carrier signal in a process called **modulation** (Fig. 11.6); the sum of the carrier and data signals is what is transmitted over the line. At the other end of the line the carrier signal is subtracted (or filtered) from the signal (**demodulation**) leaving the data. These functions are performed by a **modem** (modulator/demodulator). Normally, there is one modem at each end of a communication line.

Radio works on essentially the same principle. The radio station transmits a constant carrier signal at an assigned frequency (say, 102.7) and adds music and voice (data) to it. To tune that station, you set the radio dial to the station's frequency. Your receiver then filters out the carrier signal, leaving the data. If you set the dial to a different frequency, a different carrier signal is filtered, leaving different data. The carrier signal allows you to tune your radio to your favorite station.

Data are often transmitted using a binary code such as ASCII (the American Standard Code for Information Interchange). The transmission speed, or **baud** rate, is a function of the signal's frequency. Typically, one bit is transmitted during each cycle, so a 2400-baud line has a carrier frequency of 2400 cycles per second and can transmit 2400 bits per second.

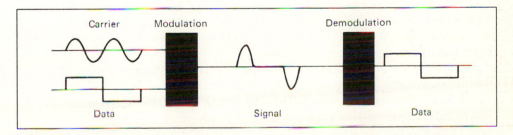

Figure 11.6   A data signal is merged with a carrier signal in a process called modulation. At the other end of the line the carrier signal is subtracted, leaving the data.

Analog and Digital Transmission

A **local** terminal or peripheral device is linked directly to a computer. Because the electronic signals must travel such a short distance, amplification and filtering are not necessary. Local data transmission is limited to a few hundred feet, however. With a **remote** device, amplification and filtering *are* necessary because of signal degradation and noise.

The data are discrete electrical pulses. The wave is a continuous analog representing the data. Analogs are used every day. The height of a column of mercury in a thermometer isn't the actual temperature; it represents temperature. The position of a needle on your automobile's control panel isn't speed but represents speed. A continuous wave passing over a communication line isn't the data, but it is analogous to the data.

Historically, communication lines worked strictly with the analog signal, amplifying it in much the same way a cassette player amplifies sound. The problem with such **analog** data transmission is quality. Just as turning up the volume on your tape deck amplifies the hiss as well as the music, amplifying an analog signal boosts the noise along with the data. The result is often poor data quality. With modern **digital** data transmission the signal is read by a digital repeater, reconstructed, and then retransmitted in almost precisely its original form. The result is much less noise and thus higher quality. Incidentally, on some dedicated digital lines, data are transmitted without a carrier signal.

Communication Systems

Communication Media

The telephone network is the best-known data communication medium. A typical voice-grade line is rated at roughly 2400 baud. High-speed, wide-band channels can transmit at rates approaching 1 million baud, and several baud rates between these two extremes are available. Early telephone lines were analog, and most local lines still are. However, as new lines are installed, most are digital. One interesting new digital technology transmits data with light waves through fiber optic cables.

Microwave data transmission is an alternative to telephone lines. Unfortunately, microwave transmission is restricted to a "line of sight." The earth, as we all know, is round; it curves. This curvature limits the range of microwaves, making expensive relay stations or communication satellites necessary (Fig. 11.7).

Considerable time could be spent discussing various communication media, but that would be needlessly confusing. Instead, the general term **line** can be used to describe any data communication medium.

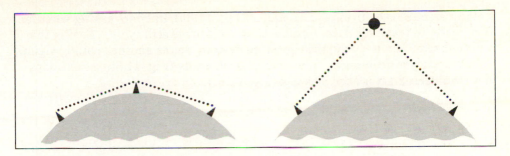

Figure 11.7 Microwave data transmission is limited to a "line of sight." Long-distance microwave transmission requires relay stations or satellites.

Protocols

Data are transmitted from a sender to a receiver following a precise set of rules called a **protocol**. For two devices to communicate, they must both follow the same rules.

You use a primitive protocol when you answer the telephone. When the phone rings, you pick up the receiver and say "hello." The caller responds with something like "Hello, this is X; may I speak to Y, please." If the desired party is not present or a wrong number has been dialed, the call quickly ends. Otherwise, communication begins. Transmission ends when both parties say "goodbye" and hang up.

Electronic devices do much the same thing when data are transmitted. First, an electronic pulse indicates that a signal is coming. Next, the sender and receiver must electronically synchronize their signals and identify each other. Data are then transmitted using a common code and baud rate. Often, the message is checked for accuracy, and, if necessary, the receiver requests retransmission. Finally, the message is acknowledged, and the transmission ends.

Network Management

A network may include numerous terminals, computers, and communication lines. Each terminal or computer may support an independent user accessing an independent program. Data intended for user A are useless to user B, so data must be routed to specific computers or terminals. Also, with multiple users active, it is inevitable that two or more will try to transmit data at the same time. Consequently, it is essential that access to the network be managed.

One way to manage the network is through a process called **polling**. Start with a user computer. As data are typed, they are stored in the user computer's memory. Eventually, the user issues a command to send the data to the central database, thus marking his or her computer "ready."

Inside the central computer the operating system has a table listing every active user computer. Referring to this table, the operating system sends a polling signal to the first user computer (Fig. 11.8a), in effect asking whether it is ready to transmit data. Assume that the user is still typing. Seeing that the computer is not ready, the operating system issues another polling signal, this time to your computer. Your computer is ready (Fig. 11.8b), so the data are transferred across the network (Fig. 11.8c).

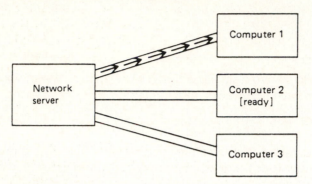

Figure 11.8(a)   A polling signal is sent to the first computer.

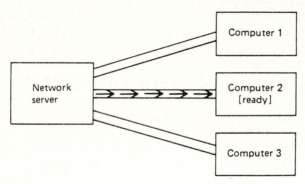

Figure 11.8(b)   Because the first computer is not ready, a polling signal is sent to the second computer.

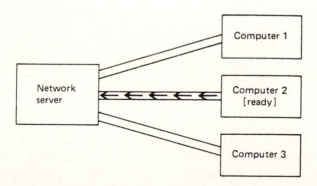

Figure 11.8(c)   Because the second computer is ready, it transmits its data to the network server.

Polling is not the only way to manage a network. In a **token passing** network an electronic signal called a token is continuously passed from computer to computer. Only the computer that holds the token is allowed to transmit data; all others must wait their turn.

With **collision detection**, on the other hand, the individual computers or terminals are allowed to transmit data whenever they want. Sophisticated electronic equipment then monitors the line, "listening" for the noise that is generated when two or more messages "collide." If a collision is detected, the affected computers retransmit in turn.

Data Communication Software

A computer can do nothing without a program to provide control. Software is needed to check protocols, manage the network, and perform other essential tasks. A microcomputer network is controlled by a **network operating system** that is usually found on the network server. Often, each user computer contains a communication program that *emulates* a terminal. The emulation software is sometimes stored in read-only memory (ROM) on a data communication board inside each user computer. Mainframe computers often assign responsibility for controlling the network to a program called **data communication monitor**. Sometimes, the necessary tasks are performed by a program on a separate microcomputer or minicomputer called a **front-end device** (Fig. 11.9).

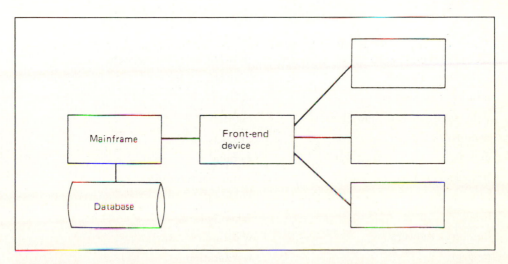

Figure 11.9 On a large computer system, network control is sometimes assigned to a front-end device.

Summary

A network is a group of computers linked by communication lines. Networks allow users to share data, hardware, and software. On many microcomputer networks, one computer, the network server, houses a central database and other shared resources. The computers that form a local area network are generally quite close to each other. The computers in a wide area network can be widely separated.

When data are transmitted over a distance, amplification and filtering are necessary because the signal tends to degrade and to pick up noise. Often, data are transmitted in the context of a carrier signal. Adding data to the carrier signal is called modulation; extracting the data is called demodulation; these tasks are performed by a modem. With analog data transmission the entire signal, including noise, is amplified. With digital data transmission the signal is reconstructed and then retransmitted. Perhaps the best-known data communication medium is the telephone network. Microwave is an alternative.

If two electronic devices are to communicate, they must follow a consistent protocol. Because conflicts are possible, access to the network must be managed by using a technique such as polling, token passing, or collision detection. Software is needed to perform these tasks. On a microcomputer network the network operating system is usually found on the network server, often with terminal emulation software on the user computers. A mainframe computer may use a data communication monitor or a front-end device.

Key Words

analog	modulation
baud	network
carrier signal	network operating system
collision detection	network server
data communication	noise
data communication monitor	polling
demodulation	protocol
digital	remote
front-end device	signal degradation
line	terminal
local	token passing
local area network	wide area network
modem	workstation

Self-Test

1. Several computers linked by communication lines form a _____.

2. On a microcomputer network the central computer that controls the network is called the _____.

3. In a _____ network, all the computers are located in a limited area.

4. A _____ network is composed of computers that are geographically dispersed.

5. When electronic signals are transmitted over a distance, they tend to _____ and pick up _____.

6. Data are normally transmitted in the context of a _____ to simplify boosting and filtering.

7. The process of adding data to a carrier signal is called _____. The process of extracting the data is called _____. These tasks are performed by a _____.

8. The basic measure of data communication speed is the _____ rate.

9. With _____ data transmission, noise is amplified along with the data. With _____ data transmission the signal is reconstructed and retransmitted.

10. If two electronic devices are to communicate successfully, they must both follow the same _____.

11. With _____, a central computer asks each user computer, in turn, if it is ready to transmit data.

12. The best-known data communication medium is the _____ .

13. On a _____ network, an electronic signal is continuously passed from computer to computer and only the machine that holds the signal is allowed to transmit.

14. On a network that uses _____ , sophisticated electronic equipment listens for the noise that is generated when two messages collide.

15. On a microcomputer network a software routine called the _____ is often stored on the network server.

Relating the Concepts

1. What is a network?

2. What advantages are derived from using a network?

3. Why is it necessary to filter and boost the signal when transmitting data over a distance?

4. What is a carrier signal? Why are carrier signals used?

5. Briefly explain modulation and demodulation.

6. Distinguish between analog and digital data transmission.
7. What is a protocol? Why are protocols necessary?
8. Briefly explain polling.
9. Briefly explain collision detection and token passing.
10. Why is network software necessary?

12

Information Systems

Preview

Computers are general-purpose machines that can be applied to a wide variety of applications. The unique requirements of a particular application are met by carefully selecting a set of hardware, software, and data components to define a computing environment. This chapter describes several common information system configurations. Key concepts include:

Small computer systems

- Personal computing
- Small group computing

Management information systems

- Business information needs
- The evolution of MIS
- Decision support systems

Scientific computing

Small Computer Systems

Personal Computing

Perhaps the most recognizable **computing environment** is a stand-alone microcomputer or **personal computer** (Fig. 12.1) intended to be used by one person at a time. A typical configuration consists of a computer, a display, a keyboard, a hard disk, a diskette drive, and a printer. Most users run word processing, spreadsheet, and database programs. Games are popular, too, and many small businesses have adopted stand-alone micros to run their office management and database applications.

By adding a modem to a personal computer the user gains access to a vast array of communication services. Electronic bulletin boards allow hobbyists all over the country to share their ideas. More specialized users can access stock market quotations, up-to-the-minute news, weather reports, and a host of other services. Some professionals use personal computers to work at home, communicating with a central office over telephone lines. Such telecommuting arrangements will become increasingly common over the next decade.

Often, several personal computers are linked to form a local area network; for example, your school might use one to manage a microcomputer laboratory. The basic idea is to store software and data on a central computer and then **download** them to user computers as required (Fig. 12.2). The network

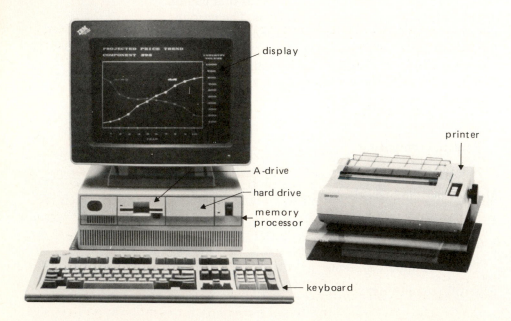

Figure 12.1   A personal computer system.

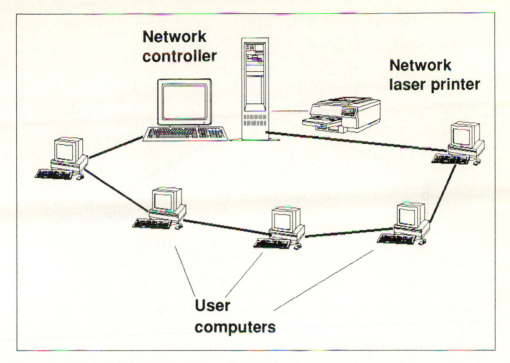

Network controller

Network laser printer

User computers

Figure 12.2 In many microcomputer labs, software and data are stored on a central computer and then downloaded over a network to user computers.

also allows the users to share hardware (such as a laser printer, a plotter, or a scanner). Other common features include electronic bulletin boards and electronic mail (E-mail). Note that, although the computers are linked, the users still work independently.

Small Group Computing

It is also possible for a local area network to support a group of people working on related tasks. For example, picture a team creating an advertising brochure or a newsletter (Fig. 12.3). Authors prepare text using a word processor and store their work on a central database. Copy editors read the authors' work and make corrections. Artists prepare illustrations to accompany the text using a graphics program. Designers use a desktop publishing program to lay out the pages, merging the text and graphics and adding captions, lines, titles, and borders.

The local area network that supports such small group applications is often built around a minicomputer. Data and software are stored on the mini's disk drives and downloaded to the workstations as needed. Printers, scanners, and other input and output devices are accessed through the central machine. Note that the hardware/software configuration defines a computing environment that effectively supports this type of application.

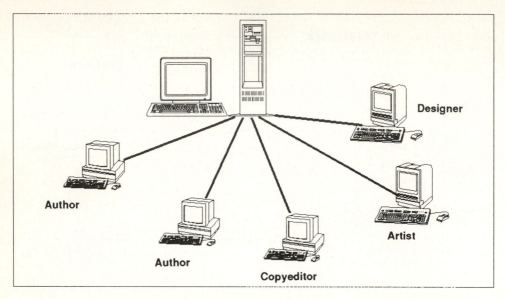

Figure 12.3 A local area network can be used to link people performing related tasks.

Small group networks have long been used to develop software, with programmers, analysts, documentation specialists, technical writers, and other professionals working on various aspects of the code. CAD/CAM (computer-aided design/computer-aided manufacturing) is another common small

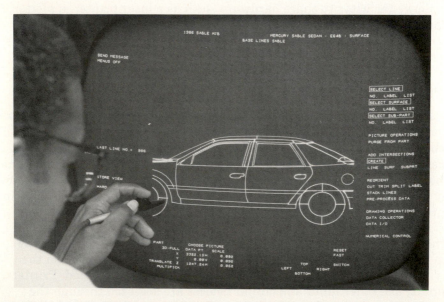

Figure 12.4 CAD/CAM has become the standard for drafting and engineering design. Courtesy of Ford Motor Company.

group application (Fig. 12.4). A network of sophisticated graphic workstations linked to a central minicomputer and running a CAD/CAM program has become almost the norm in drafting and engineering design.

Management Information Systems

Although personal computers and small group networks are common in big business, most corporate computing is done on mainframe systems. Perhaps the best way to gain an understanding of a modern business computing environment is first to consider the kinds of information required by business people.

Business Information Needs

A typical business organizational structure resembles a pyramid (Fig. 12.5). Like a military chain of command, authority and responsibility flow from the

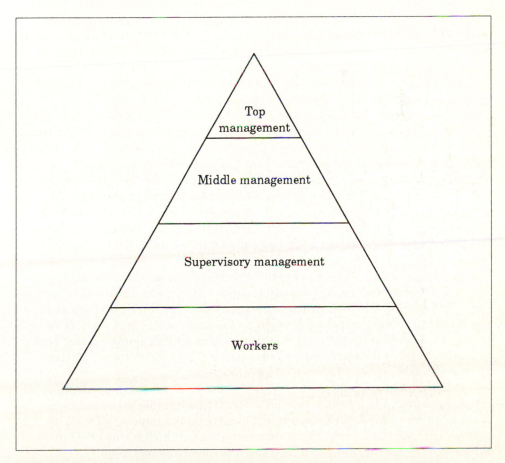

Figure 12.5 A typical business organization structure resembles a pyramid.

Management level	Top	Middle	Supervisory
Decision type	Strategic	Tactical	Operational
Decision characteristics	Unstructured Unprogrammed	Semistructured	Structured Programmed
Degree of uncertainty	High	Intermediate	Low
Time frame	Future	Near future	Current
Type of information	Highly summarized	Summarized	Detailed

Figure 12.6 The type of information required by a manager depends on that individual's job.

top, down. Like generals, the top managers make strategic decisions. Under them come the middle managers who, like captains and majors, make the tactical decisions needed to carry out top management's strategy. Below them are the supervisors who, like lieutenants, make the day-by-day operational decisions needed to control the people who do the actual work.

Information needs vary with management level. For example, start with the supervisors (Fig. 12.6). Because they are responsible for day-to-day operations, they need detailed, current information. In most cases they rely on standard operating procedures, so their decisions tend to be highly structured, almost programmed. Supervisors are rarely asked to deal with uncertainty; their job is see that a specified unit of work is done on time.

Middle managers, on the other hand, make near-future tactical decisions (Fig. 12.6). Top management's strategic objectives provide a structure for these decisions, but because there may be several different ways to achieve their objectives, middle managers face some uncertainty. Instead of detailed data, they need summarized data. Instead of current data, they need near-future projections.

Top management defines the organization's long-term strategic objectives (Fig. 12.6). Consequently, top management needs projections based on highly summarized data. Because strategic decisions depend in part on factors beyond the organization's control (such as the state of the economy), they involve considerable uncertainty. Long-term planning depends a great deal on the top managers' intuitions and visions, so these decisions are unstructured and unprogrammed.

A modern business information system must meet all these needs, providing supervisors with detailed, current information, middle managers with summaries and near-future projections, and top management with highly summarized information and long-term projections. Such complex systems did not simply spring into being. Instead, they evolved over time.

The Evolution of MIS

The summaries and projections required by middle and top-level management are derived from detailed current data, so the detailed data must come first. Consequently, it is not surprising that early business computing environments, often called **electronic data processing (EDP)** systems, worked almost exclusively with current details.

For example, consider the payroll application (Fig. 12.7). During the week, employees report their hours worked by punching a time clock. At the end of the week, the labor data are collected, checked, and carried to the computer center. At a prescheduled time, the data are read into a payroll program that uses the current week's data to compute current earnings, reads last week's year-to-date earnings from a magnetic tape or disk file, and adds current income to get the new year-to-date totals. Outputs include a new year-to-date file, current paychecks, and several payroll reports.

This mode of operation, called **batch processing**, was common during the electronic data processing era. Sales reports were compiled by collecting sales slips, entering the data into the computer at the end of the day or the end of the week, and then organizing the data by salesperson, by office, by region,

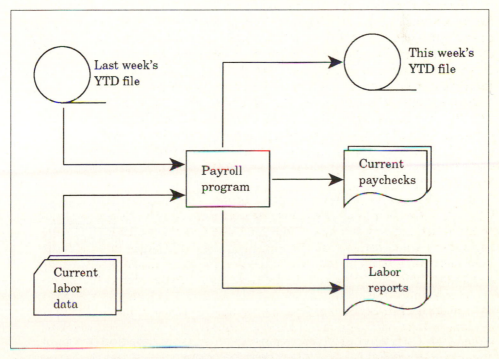

Figure 12.7 Payroll is a typical electronic data processing application.

and so on. Inventory status reports were generated by collecting the paperwork on products added to and deleted from inventory and then using these data to update last week's or last month's stock levels. Other similar applications included accounts payable, accounts receivable, general ledger, billing, and a host of other accounting tasks.

The problem with batch processing is that the data are not current. (Printed reports, by their very nature, are out of date almost as soon as they are printed.) A significant improvement came with the development of **transaction processing** systems (Fig. 12.8). On a batch processing system, paperwork is collected, sent to a central site, and then input to the computer. On a transaction processing system, the data that describe an event are entered through an on-line terminal as the event occurs. Consequently, the data stored on the computer are much more up to date. For example, there is a significant difference between knowing what was in the warehouse a week ago and knowing what is in the warehouse right now. Transaction processing gave supervisors the current information they needed.

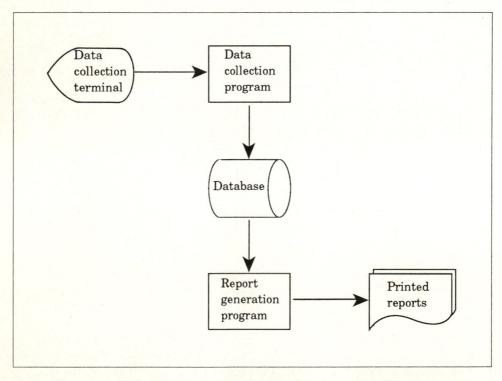

Figure 12.8 On a transaction processing system, data are collected and input through a terminal as the events they describe happen. Consequently, the data are more current.

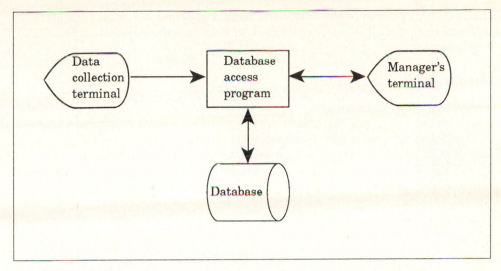

Figure 12.9 On a management information system, middle managers can access and even manipulate current data through on-line terminals.

The next step was to allow middle management to access the current data. The development of database management systems was one key. The evolution of terminal networks allowed management to access data from their desks. New software made it possible to create special reports and actually manipulate the data. The result (Fig. 12.9) was a **management information system** (**MIS**) that supported tactical, middle-management decision making.

Management information systems changed the nature of business computation. Instead of merely tracking and summarizing paperwork, a computer in the hands of a clever manager could be used to give the company a competitive advantage. For example, imagine that a customer has just placed a large order but requires delivery in 30 days. A manager working in an electronic data processing environment might have to wait until new inventory and production status reports are printed at the end of the week before committing to a delivery schedule. However, given a management information system, that manager can extract the relevant information from the current inventory and production databases and give the customer a firm delivery date almost immediately.

In the old days, an organization's computer center was housed in a glass-enclosed, climate-controlled room. Access was strictly limited to those with a need to know, so **security** was not a serious problem. However, the widely disbursed on-line terminals common to management information systems complicate physical access control. In effect, anyone with a terminal and a modem can potentially access the firm's most sensitive data, particularly if the network relies on public telephone lines. Consequently, improved security and access controls became a priority, and they remain serious problems even today.

Decision Support Systems

The next step in the evolution of business computation is likely to involve the development of sophisticated **decision support systems (DSS)**. Electronic data processing gives supervisors the current data they need. Management information systems make the data available to middle managers and provide facilities to support tactical decision making. Decision support systems include additional features needed by top management for strategic decision making.

A management information system serves as the base. Replace the terminals with networked microcomputers or intelligent workstations, and you give the users a great deal of new computational power. For example, those microcomputers allow a manager to perform sophisticated **"what if" analysis**, obtaining current information from the central database, making different assumptions, and using the computer to manipulate the data and project the outcome based on those assumptions. "What if" analysis allows the manager to "try out" various tactics and strategies before reaching a final decision, and that improves decision making.

Spreadsheets are popular decision support tools. Once a spreadsheet model is properly set up, the user can quickly recompute its cells by changing only one or two values. Many decision support systems also include sophisticated mathematical and simulation models, and future versions are likely to incorporate artificial intelligence.

Scientific Computing

Most business computing tasks are **I/O bound**; in other words, the computer spends more time reading and writing data than processing those data. **Scientific computation** is different. For example, consider the task of simulating a nuclear reaction. The amount of input data is limited, but extensive computation is required to track the rapidly changing physical state of the material. Because such tasks require much more computation time than I/O time, they are said to be **compute bound**.

Typical scientific applications include data collection (Fig. 12.10), statistical data analysis, number crunching (solving complex equations), and simulation. Most of these functions can be performed by a general-purpose computer, but the unique demands of scientific computing sometimes call for a stand-alone system. For example, a computer collecting **real-time** data from a piece of scientific equipment might have to respond within microseconds. Because most general-purpose mainframes run several programs concurrently, that response time might be impossible to maintain. However, if a

Figure 12.10 Scientific data collection often calls for a stand-alone micro- or minicomputer. Courtesy of MLS/A-Dan Murray.

stand-alone micro- or minicomputer is dedicated to the task, the necessary response time can be guaranteed.

Another problem on some applications is the sheer volume of computation. For example, imagine tracking a space shuttle launch. The equations that account for such variables as lift, thrust, wind velocity, wind direction, the earth's rotation, and numerous others are quite complex. As the vehicle begins to rise, those equations must be solved very quickly so that minor corrections can be made to adjust for changing conditions. That calls for a fast, dedicated computer.

Most general-purpose computers have large instruction sets that support binary, fixed-point, and floating-point arithmetic as well as string manipulation, but a typical scientific program uses only a handful of those instructions. The arithmetic and logic unit of a **reduced instruction set computer (RISC)** is designed with a limited repertoire of highly efficient instructions, so programs run faster. RISC machines are used for many scientific applications, particularly those calling for high-resolution graphics.

The fastest computers, sometimes called **supercomputers**, are specifically designed for scientific computation. They run perhaps an order of magnitude faster than the most powerful general-purpose mainframes. Additional speed and precision are gained by using a larger word size, and they often execute several instructions in parallel. These supercomputers are generally found in large research laboratories.

Summary

A computer is a general-purpose machine. To support a particular set of applications, components are carefully selected to define a computing environment. Personal computer systems are designed to be used by one person at a time. Often, several personal computers are linked by a network, and software and data are downloaded from a central computer as required. Local area networks are also used to support small group computing, with user workstations linked to a central minicomputer.

A business information system must support operational, tactical, and strategic decision making. Early electronic data processing systems relied on batch processing applications to maintain detailed current data. Transaction processing provided more timely data. A management information system allows middle managers to access the data and use them to support tactical decision making, but on-line terminals create security problems. A decision support system allows top-level management to perform the "what if" analysis needed for strategic decision making.

Most business applications are I/O bound, but scientific computation is characterized by compute bound programs. Often, scientific applications call for a dedicated computer, particularly when the task requires a real-time response. A reduced instruction set computer is faster than a comparable general-purpose machine. Supercomputers are used to solve large scientific problems.

Key Words

batch processing	personal computer
compute bound	real-time
computing environment	reduced instruction set computer (RISC)
decision support system (DSS)	scientific computation
download	security
electronic data processing (EDP)	supercomputer
I/O bound	transaction processing
management information system (MIS)	"what if" analysis

Self-Test

1. A set of hardware, software, and data components defines a computing _____ that supports a particular class of applications.

2. A _____ computer system is intended to be used by one person at a time.

3. On a local area network, software and data are stored on a central computer and _____ to user computers as required.

4. On a small group network, data and software are sometimes downloaded to user _____ from a central minicomputer.

5. Supervisors make _____ decisions. Middle managers make _____ decisions. Top-level managers make _____ decisions.

6. Supervisors require _____ information about current conditions, while top management requires _____ information and future projections.

7. On a _____ processing application, data are collected and subsequently input to a computer at a scheduled time.

8. On a _____ processing application, the data that describe an event are input when that event occurs.

9. A _____ makes current data available to middle managers and provides enough data manipulation capability to support tactical decision making.

10. A management information system's on-line terminals create _____ problems.

11. A decision support system allows a manager to perform the _____ analysis needed for strategic decision making.

12. Most business applications are _____, spending more time reading and writing data than processing data. Many scientific applications are _____, spending more time on computations than on input and output.

13. Scientific applications sometimes call for a dedicated computer because they require _____ response.

14. A _____ computer is faster than a general-purpose computer because it supports a limited number of highly efficient instructions.

15. Large scientific problems are often solved on a _____.

Relating the Concepts

1. What are the characteristics that distinguish a personal computer from other types of computers?

2. Briefly explain the advantages associated with storing data and software on a central computer and downloading them to user computers as required.

3. Distinguish between operational, tactical, and strategic decision making. How does the type of decision influence the type of data required by the decision maker?

4. Distinguish between batch processing and transaction processing.

5. Distinguish between an electronic data processing system, a management information system, and a decision support system. Relate these concepts to operational, tactical, and strategic decision making.

6. Briefly explain "what if" analysis. Why is it so valuable?

7. Distinguish between I/O bound and compute bound applications.

8. Scientific applications sometimes call for a dedicated computer. Why?

9. What is a RISC machine? What is a supercomputer?

10. Briefly explain how the computing environment influences the kinds of applications a system can support.

Number Systems and Data Types

Number Systems

Decimal Numbers

A decimal number consists of a series of digits—0, 1, 2, 3, 4, 5, 6, 7, 8, 9—written in precise relative positions. The value of a given number is found by multiplying each digit by its place or positional value and adding the products. For example, the number 3582 represents:

```
  3 times  1000 = 3000
+ 5 times   100 =  500
+ 8 times    10 =   80
+ 2 times     1 =    2
                 _____
                   3582
```

Generally, the value of any number is the sum of the products of its digit and place values.

Take a close look at the decimal place values 1, 10, 100, 1000, 10,000, and so on. The pattern is obvious. Rather than writing all those zeros, you can use scientific notation—for example, writing 10,000 as 10^4. Because any number raised to the zero power is 1, you can write the decimal place values as the base (10) raised to a series of integer powers:

$$... \quad 10^8 \quad 10^7 \quad 10^6 \quad 10^5 \quad 10^4 \quad 10^3 \quad 10^2 \quad 10^1 \quad 10^0$$

A few general rules can be derived from this discussion of decimal numbers. First is the idea of place or positional value represented by the base (10) raised to a series of integer powers. The second is the use of the digit zero (0) to represent "nothing" in a given position. (How else could you distinguish 3 from 30?) Finally, only values less than the base (in this case, 10) can be written with a single digit, so a total of ten digits (0 through 9) is needed to write decimal values.

Binary Numbers

There is nothing to restrict the application of these rules to a base-10 number system. If the positional values are powers of 2, you have the framework of a binary or base-2 number system:

$$... \quad 2^8 \quad 2^7 \quad 2^6 \quad 2^5 \quad 2^4 \quad 2^3 \quad 2^2 \quad 2^1 \quad 2^0$$

As in any number system, the digit zero (0) is needed to represent nothing in a given position. Additionally, the binary number system needs only one other digit, 1. Given this structure, you can find the value of any binary number by multiplying each digit by its place value and adding the products. For example, the binary number 1100011 is:

$$
\begin{aligned}
& 1 \text{ times } 2^6 = 1 \text{ times } \ 64 = 64 \\
+\ & 1 \text{ times } 2^5 = 1 \text{ times } \ 32 = 32 \\
+\ & 0 \text{ times } 2^4 = 0 \text{ times } \ 16 = \ \ 0 \\
+\ & 0 \text{ times } 2^3 = 0 \text{ times } \ \ \ 8 = \ \ 0 \\
+\ & 0 \text{ times } 2^2 = 0 \text{ times } \ \ \ 4 = \ \ 0 \\
+\ & 1 \text{ times } 2^1 = 1 \text{ times } \ \ \ 2 = \ \ 2 \\
+\ & 1 \text{ times } 2^0 = 1 \text{ times } \ \ \ 1 = \ \ 1 \\
\hline
& \qquad\qquad\qquad\qquad\qquad\qquad 99
\end{aligned}
$$

The decimal number 2 is 10 in binary; the decimal number 4 is 100. Decimal 5 is 101 (1 four, 0 two's, and 1 one).

Octal and Hexadecimal

Other number systems, notably octal (base 8) and hexadecimal (base 16), are commonly used with computers. The octal number system uses powers of 8 to represent positional values and the digit values 0, 1, 2, 3, 4, 5, 6, and 7. The hexadecimal number system uses powers of 16 and the digits 0, 1, 2, 3, 4, 5, 6, 7, 8, 9, A, B, C, D, E, and F. The hexadecimal number FF is:

$$
\begin{aligned}
& 15 \text{ times } 16^1 = 240 \\
+\ & 15 \text{ times } 16^0 = \ \ 15 \\
\hline
& \qquad\qquad\qquad\quad 255
\end{aligned}
$$

There are *no* computers that work directly with octal or hex; a computer is a *binary* machine. Octal and hex are used simply because it is easy to convert between them and binary. Each octal digit is exactly equivalent to three binary digits; each hexadecimal digit is exactly equivalent to four binary digits. Thus octal and hex can be used as shorthands for displaying binary values.

Data Types

Numeric Data

Because binary numbers are so well suited to electronic devices, computers are at their most efficient when working with pure binary. A typical computer is designed around a basic unit of data called a word (usually 8, 16, or 32 bits). The high-order bit holds a sign (0 for +, 1 for –); the remaining bits hold data. There is no provision for a decimal point; decimal point alignment is the programmer's responsibility. The biggest binary value that can be stored on a 32-bit word computer is

01111111111111111111111111111111

or 2,147,483,647 in decimal. The limit on a 16-bit machine is

0111111111111111

which is 32,767 in decimal.

Binary integers won't do for very large, very small, and fractional numbers. With scientific notation, numbers are written as a decimal fraction followed by a power of 10; for example, the speed of light, 186,000 miles per second, is expressed in scientific form as 0.186×10^6. Many computers can store and manipulate binary approximations of scientific numbers called floating-point or real numbers.

Certain applications, particularly business applications, demand precisely rounded decimal numbers. While any data type will do for whole numbers or integers, floating-point and binary provide at best a close approximation to decimal fractions, so many computers support a form of decimal data. Generally, computers are at their least efficient when processing decimal data.

String Data

Many applications call for such nonnumeric data as names, addresses, and product descriptions. These string values are typically stored as sets of individual characters, each character being represented by a code such as ASCII or EBCDIC (see Chapter 2, Fig. 2.6). Typically, a single coded character occupies one byte. The name "Jones," for example, would be stored in five consecutive bytes.

It is important to note that strings and numbers are different. For example, if you type the digit 1 followed by the digit 2, each character will be stored in memory as a 1-byte string. On a computer that uses the ASCII code, these two characters would appear as:

    01010001   01010010

That's *not* the number 12. On a 16-bit computer a pure binary 12 is stored as

    0000000000001100

(Try using the "digit-times-place-value" rule.) Numbers and strings are different. That's why, in most programming languages, you must distinguish strings from numbers. The positional value of each digit in a number is significant. The positional values of the individual bits have no meaning in a string.

Number System Exercises

1. Convert the following binary numbers to decimal.

   a. 1000   *8*   g. 11100   *28*
   b. 1100   *12*   h. 10011   *19*
   c. 0111   *7*   i. 100100 *36*
   d. 1111   *15*   j. 111000 *56*
   e. 10000 *16*   k. 101010 *42*
   f. 10101 *21*   l. 100111 *39*

2. Count to 16 in binary.

3. Briefly explain the difference between string data and numeric data. Why is this difference important?

B

Answers to Chapter Self-Tests

Chapter 1

1. data
   information
2. data
   information
3. input
   output
4. stored program
5. ENIAC
6. tube
   transistors
   integrated circuits
7. artificial intelligence
8. memory
   processor
9. hardware
10. software

Chapter 2

1. two
2. hardware
   software
3. byte
   word
4. code
5. numbers
   characters
6. address
7. read
   written
8. RAM
   ROM
9. instructions
10. operation code
    operands

12. direct, or random
13. redundancy
14. dependency
15. database management system

Chapter 9

1. system
2. systems analyst
3. problem definition
4. user
5. feasibility study
6. logical
7. data flow diagrams
   data dictionary
   algorithm descriptions
8. design
9. system flowchart
10. sequential
11. direct, or random
12. debug
13. documentation
14. implementation
15. maintenance

Chapter 10

1. waiting for I/O
2. multiprogramming
3. concurrent
4. operating system
5. dispatcher
6. interrupts
7. wait
8. fixed-partition

9. dynamic
10. virtual
11. queue
12. scheduler
13. Spooling
14. time-sharing
15. multiprocessing

Chapter 11

1. network
2. network server
3. local area
4. wide area
5. lose intensity
   noise
6. carrier signal
7. modulation
   demodulation
   modem
8. baud
9. analog
   digital
10. protocol
11. polling
12. telephone network
13. token passing
14. collision detection
15. network operating system

Chapter 12

1. environment
2. personal
3. downloaded
4. workstations

5. operational
   tactical
   strategic
6. detailed
   highly summarized
7. batch
8. transaction
9. management information system
10. security
11. "what if"
12. I/O bound
    compute bound
13. real-time
14. RISC
15. supercomputer

Appendix A

1. a. 8
   b. 12
   c. 7
   d. 15
   e. 16
   f. 21
   g. 28
   h. 19
   i. 36
   j. 56
   k. 42
   l. 39
2. 1, 10, 11, 100, 101, 110, 111, 1000, 1001, 1010, 1011, 1100, 1101, 1110, 1111, 10000

Glossary

This glossary contains brief definitions that are intended to convey a sense of the meanings of selected key words. For more precise definitions, see:

The American National Dictionary for Information Processing, American National Standards Institute, 1430 Broadway, New York, New York 10018.

The ISO Vocabulary of Data Processing, published by The International Organization for Standardization, 1 rue de Varemde, Case Postale 56, CH–1121, Geneva 20, Switzerland.

Access mechanism On disk, the part that holds the read/write head. Like the tone arm on a stereo turntable, the access mechanism moves to position the read/write head over the track containing the desired data.

Access method A software routine that translates a programmer's logical request for input or output into the physical commands required by the external device.

Address A location in memory. Often, the bytes or words that make up memory are numbered sequentially; the byte's (or word's) number is its address.

Algorithm A rule or a set of rules for arriving at an answer in a finite number of steps.

Analog Data represented in a continuous physical form. The height of a column of mercury is an analog representation of a temperature. Computer data are transmitted over local telephone lines by converting them to continuous wave form. Contrast with *Digital*.

Analysis The step in the systems analysis and design process during which a systems analyst determines what must be done to solve a problem and develops a logical system plan.

Application program A program written to perform an end user task. A payroll program or a computer game is an application program; an operating system is not. Contrast with *System software*.

Architecture See *Computer architecture*.

Arithmetic and logic unit The part of a computer's processor that executes instructions.

Array A data structure in which memory is allocated as a series of numbered cells. Individual data elements can be placed in or extracted from one of these cells by referring to the cell's number or numbers.

Artificial intelligence The characteristics of a nonorganic system that are usually associated with human intelligence.

Assembler A programming language in which one mnemonic source statement is coded for each machine-level instruction.

Backup Extra hardware, software, or data that are intended to keep a computer system running in the event that one or more components fail.

Base In a number system, the number used to define positional values. For example, decimal uses base 10, while binary uses 2 as its base.

Batch processing A type of computer application in which data are collected over time and then processed together. For example, payroll data might be collected throughout the week and processed on Friday. Contrast with *Transaction processing*.

Baud The basic unit of data communication speed measured in discrete signal events per second, often bits per second.

Binary A base-2 number system that uses values 0 and 1.

Bit A binary digit.

Boot A small routine, read into main memory when the computer is activated, that loads the rest of the operating system.

Bug An error in a program.

Bus A set of parallel wires used to transmit data, commands, or power.

Byte Eight bits. On many computer systems, the smallest addressable unit of memory.

Cable An electrical connector; often, a shielded, serial wire.

Carrier signal A standard, predictable signal, such as a sine wave, used to transmit data. The unaltered signal indicates an absence of data; alterations in the pattern convey meaning.

CD-ROM Acronym for compact-disk read-only

storage. A high-capacity read-only secondary storage medium.

Central processing unit See *Processor*.

Channel A device used to attach input, output, and secondary storage devices to a large computer system. The channel contains its own processor and thus can free the main processor from responsibility for controlling I/O operations.

Character A single letter, digit, or other symbol. On many computers, each byte of memory can hold a single character in coded form.

Clock A device that generates the regular electronic pulses that drive a computer.

Code (1) A set of rules for representing characters as bit patterns. (2) To write a program.

Coding The act of writing a program.

Collision detection A network management technique in which electronic devices monitor the line, listen for the noise that is generated when two messages collide, and order the affected

terminals to retransmit when collisions are detected.

Command (1) A control signal that tells a hardware component to perform a function. For example, a fetch command tells memory to transfer the contents of a single memory location to a bus, and a seek command tells a disk interface to position the access mechanism (2) A request from a programmer, an operator, or a user to an operating system asking that a function be performed— for example, a request to load a program.

Command driven A software routine that relies on commands as its driving mechanism. For example, MS/DOS is a command-driven operating system.

Command language A language for communicating with an operating system.

Command processor An operating system module that reads, interprets, and carries out commands.

Commercial software Purchased, ready-to-use software. Contrast with custom software or original software.

Compiler A support program that reads a source program, translates the source statements to machine language, and outputs a complete binary object program. Contrast with *Interpreter*.

Compute bound An application that requires more computation than input or output.

Computer A machine that processes data into information under control of a stored program.

Computer architecture The physical structure of a computer; in particular, the way in which a computer's components are linked.

Computer program A series of instructions that guides a computer through a process.

Computing environment A configuration of hardware, software, and data that supports a particular set of applications.

Concurrent Over the same time period.

Control unit, instruction See *Instruction control unit*.

Control unit, I/O An electronic device that

links an I/O device to a channel.

CPU Acronym for *Central processing unit.*

Cursor The blinking line or box that indicates where the next character typed or output will appear on a display screen.

Cycle Any set of operations that are repeated regularly in the same order. In data communications, one complete "S-on-its-side" sine wave represents a single cycle.

Cylinder On a multisurface disk pack, one position of the access mechanism that defines a set of several tracks.

Data Raw, unstructured, unprocessed facts.

Database A collection of related data. Generally, an integrated, centralized collection of an organization's data.

Database management system Software and/or hardware that controls access to a database.

Data communication Transmitting data over a communication line.

Data communication monitor A software routine or program that controls or monitors the data communication process.

Data dependency A condition that occurs when a program's logic is excessively dependent on its physical data structure. Data-dependent programs are difficult to maintain.

Data dictionary A collection of data about the data.

Data element A single, meaningful unit of data.

Data flow diagram A graphic representation of a logical system showing how data flow between sources, processes, stores, and destinations.

Data management Storing data in such a way that they can be retrieved when needed.

Data processing Converting data into information.

Data set See *Modem.*

Data structure An organized set of data. Examples include a list, an array, and a file.

Debug To remove errors (bugs) from a program.

Decision support system A computer-based system with facilities to support top-level, strategic decision making.

Declarative language See *Nonprocedural language.*

Demodulation The reverse of modulation. Conversion of data from analog to digital form.

Design The step in the systems analysis and design process during which an analyst develops a physical design for the system.

Desktop publishing A computer application that allows a user to format a printed page, integrating text and graphics.

Digital Data represented as individual, discrete digits. Contrast with *Analog.*

Direct access Accessing data without regard for its physical position in a file or on disk. Contrast with *Sequential access.*

Directory A list of files stored on a disk or some other secondary medium.

Disk, magnetic A flat, platelike surface on which data can be stored magnetically.

Diskette A thin, flexible magnetic disk that is

often used on small computer systems. Also called a floppy disk.

Disk pack A set of two or more disks stacked on a common drive shaft and accessed by a common set of read/write heads.

Dispatcher The operating system module that determines which program in memory will access the processor next.

Display, or display screen A TV-like screen that displays data.

Documentation Diagrams, comments, and other materials that explain or clarify a program.

Download To copy software or data from a central computer to a personal computer or a workstation over a network.

Dynamic memory management Allocation of memory space as the space is needed.

Electronic data processing (EDP) An early type of business information system in which batch processing applications were used to maintain detailed current data.

Execution The act of carrying out an instruction or performing a routine.

Execution time, or E-time The time during which an instruction is executed by the arithmetic and logic unit.

Expert system A computer program that simulates the actions and/or thought processes of a human expert.

Feasibility study A study performed early in the system analysis and design process and aimed at determining whether the problem can be solved.

Fetch To locate a unit of data or an instruction in memory and send it over a bus to the processor.

Field A single, meaningful data element in a file.

Fifth-generation language A program language that incorporates artificial intelligence and natural language processing.

File A collection of related records.

First-generation computer A 1950s-era computer characterized by electronic tube components.

First-generation language Binary machine language.

Fixed partition memory management A memory management technique in which the available memory space is divided into fixed-length partitions.

Floppy disk See *Diskette*.

Flowchart A graphic representation of a program in which symbols represent logical steps and flowlines define the sequence of those steps.

Fourth-generation language See *Nonprocedural language*.

Front-end device A transmission control unit that links a number of communication lines to a computer system. Often, the front-end device contains considerable intelligence.

Giga Billions; for example, gigabytes.

Graphics Computer output in the form of points, lines, and shapes.

Hard disk A rigid disk. Contrast with *Diskette*. Generally, a hard disk spins constantly; consequently, data access is much faster

182

than with diskette. Also, hard disk has a greater data storage capacity.

Hardware   Physical equipment. Contrast with *Software*.

Implementation   The step in the systems analysis and design process during which the system is tested and installed   Implementation ends with the release of the program or system to a user.

Index   A value or set of values, such as an index register, a subscript, or a table used to locate specific data elements.

Information   The meaning that a human being assigns to data. Processed data.

Information processing   See *Data processing*.

Input   Transferring data from an external device into a computer's memory.

Input/output control system (IOCS)   The operating system module that is responsible for communicating directly with input, output, and secondary storage devices.

Instruction   One step in a program. Each instruction tells the computer to perform one of its basic functions.

Instruction control unit   The part of a computer's processor that decides which instruction will be executed next.

Instruction counter   A register that holds the address of the next instruction to be executed.

Instruction register   A register that holds the instruction being executed by the processor.

Instruction set   The electronic circuits that add, subtract, multiply, divide, copy, compare, request input, and request output. On most computers these are the circuits that make up the arithmetic and logic unit.

Instruction time, or I-time   The time during which the next instruction is fetched from main memory and interpreted by the processor's instruction control unit.

Interface   On a small computer, an electronic component that links an external device to a computer. More generally, an electronic component that links two devices.

Interpreter   A support program that reads a single source statement, translates it into machine language, executes the machine-level instructions, and then moves on to the next source statement. Contrast with *Compiler*.

Interrupt   An electronic signal that causes a computer to stop what it is doing and transfer control to the operating system in such a way that the task being performed at the time of the interrupt can later be resumed.

I/O   Input/output.

I/O bound   An application that requires more input and/or output than computation.

I/O control unit   See *Control unit, I/O*.

I/O device allocation   See *Peripheral device allocation*.

K   Abbreviation for kilo; 1024 bytes or words.

Keyboard   An input device on which characters are represented as discrete keys. When a key is pressed, the associated character is input to the computer system.

Line   A communication medium.

List structure A list of data elements separated by commas, semicolons, or some other separator character.

Local Connected to a computer by cables. In close proximity to the computer. Contrast with *Remote*.

Local area network A network in which all the computers are in close proximity to each other. A network that does *not* use common carrier or public communication media.

Logical I/O Input or output operations performed without regard for the physical structure of the data.

Logical system A system design that focuses on what must be done but does not specify how to do it.

Machine cycle The basic operating cycle of a processor during which a single instruction is fetched, interpreted, and executed.

Machine language Binary instructions that can be stored in memory, fetched, and executed by a computer.

Magnetic disk See *Disk, magnetic*.

Magnetic drum A cylinder that is coated on the outside surface with a magnetic material. Data are stored around the outer surface and accessed by a series of read/write heads, one head per track. A very fast medium with limited storage capacity. The first significant secondary storage medium.

Magnetic media Input, output, or secondary storage media that represent data as magnetic patterns.

Magnetic tape A popular backup medium. A ribbon of mylar coated with magnetic material. Data are recorded along the tape's surface.

Mainframe The processor of a large computer system or the set of components contained in the same physical cabinet as the processor of a large computer system.

Main memory, or main storage Memory that can be directly accessed by the processor.

Main processor On a multiprocessing computer, the primary processor. Sometimes used as a synonym for *Processor*.

Maintenance Continuing support of a program or a system after it has been released.

Management information system (MIS) A computer-based system that allows management to access and manipulate current data to support tactical decision making.

Mega Millions; for example, megabytes.

Memory The computer component in which instructions and data are stored.

Memory management Allocating memory to application programs, a task usually performed by the operating system.

Menu A list of choices.

Microcomputer A small computer system.

Microprocessor A processor on a single integrated circuit chip. The processor in a microcomputer system.

Microsecond One millionth of one second.

Microwave An electromagnetic wave used to transmit data.

Millisecond One thousandth of one second.

Minicomputer A digital computer, smaller than a mainframe but bigger than a microcomputer.

Modem An acronym for MOdulator-DEModulator. A device that converts data from the computer's internal digital form to analog wave form and back again. Used to link computer equipment to a telephone line.

Modulation Conversion of data from digital to analog.

Monitor See *Display*.

Motherboard A metal or plastic framework that holds a computer's circuit boards. Often, circuit boards slide into slots on the framework and are electronically linked by bus lines.

MS/DOS A popular microcomputer operating system.

Multiple-bus architecture A computer architecture in which multiple bus lines link components. Often, separate bus lines are provided for commands, addresses, and data.

Multiprocessing Two or more independent processors sharing a common memory.

Multiprogramming One computer concurrently executing several programs.

Nanosecond One billionth of one second.

Natural language processing Communicating with a human being in human terms.

Network Two or more computers linked by communication lines.

Network operating system The software that controls a network.

Network server The computer that controls a network. Often, a central database is accessed through the network server.

Noise In data communications, electronic interference.

Nonprocedural language A programming language in which the programmer describes the logical structure of a problem instead of writing a procedure to solve it. Also called a fourth-generation language or a declarative language.

Object module A machine-level translation of a programmer's source code.

Open To prepare a file for processing. For example, opening a file on disk involves checking the directory to find the track and sectors where the file's data are stored.

Operand The portion of an instruction that specifies the registers and/or memory locations that are to participate in the operation.

Operating system A collection of program modules that control the operation of the computer. A typical operating system allocates resources, schedules programs, controls access to input and output devices, and manages data.

Operation code The portion of an instruction that specifies the operation to be performed; for example, add, subtract, etc.

Optical media Generally, input media on which data are represented as light and dark patterns that can be interpreted by an optical scanner.

Output The act of transferring data or information from the computer's memory to an external device.

Packaged software See *Commercial software*.

Parallel Side by side. Parallel processing involves performing two or more tasks at the same time. Parallel data transmission involves sending bits, side by side, over parallel wires. Contrast with *Serial*.

Peripheral device allocation The task (usually performed by the operating system) of allocating input, output, and secondary storage devices.

Peripheral hardware Input, output, and secondary storage devices that are attached to a computer system.

Personal computer A small, inexpensive microcomputer system that is marketed for use by individuals.

Physical I/O The act of transferring a physical block of data to or from a peripheral device. For example, on diskette, each physical I/O operation might transfer one sector; on a printer, each physical I/O operation might transfer one line.

Physical system A system design that identifies specific

physical components, such as programs, input and output devices, secondary storage devices, other hardware, data files, data flows, media, and procedures.

Picosecond One millionth of one millionth of a second.

Pixel A picture element. A spot on a display screen that can be selectively turned on or off. The basic unit of a graphic display.

Polling Asking a series of terminals, or checking a series of buffers, one by one, to see whether they have data to transmit. A technique for determining who gets to transmit data next.

Primitive command A machine-level hardware command; for example, a fetch command whereby a processor requests data from memory or a seek command whereby a disk interface is told to position the access mechanism.

Printer A device that outputs printed characters.

Problem definition The first step in the systems analysis and design process during which the

analyst identifies the user's needs.

Processing (1) Executing instructions. (2) Converting data into information.

Processor The component of a computer that selects and executes instructions. The processor contains a clock, an instruction control unit, an arithmetic and logic unit, and registers.

Processor management The task of allocating the processor's time. Usually performed by the operating system.

Program See *Computer program*.

Programmer A person who writes computer programs.

Prompt A brief message that is printed or displayed by a program or by the operating system asking the user to provide input.

Protocol A set of rules for establishing communication between two devices.

Punched card An input medium that represents data as patterns of holes in a card.

Queuing Placing application programs on

a waiting line (or queue) for eventual loading into main memory.

Query language A feature of several database management systems that allows a user to extract data by asking questions.

RAM (random access memory) Memory that can be directly addressed, read, and written by the programmer. The main memory of a computer is generally RAM. Contrast with *ROM*.

Random access See *Direct access*.

Read/write head The component that transfers data to or from the surface of disk or magnetic tape.

Real-time A response time fast enough to affect current operations.

Record A collection of related fields.

Reduced instruction set computer (RISC) A computer with an instruction set that consists of a limited number of highly efficient instructions.

Redundant data Data that are repeated in two or more places.

Register Temporary storage used to hold data, instructions, or control information in the processor. Often, the current instruction, the data being manipulated by that instruction, and key control information are stored in registers.

Relative address An address relative to a reference point; for example, the tenth byte away from the beginning of a program or the third record in a file.

Relative record number The location of a record relative to the beginning of a file; for example, the fourth record in a file. Given the actual track and sector of the first record in the file, it is possible to compute the address of any other record given its relative record number.

Remote Distant. Linked to a computer by communication lines. Contrast with *Local*.

Requirements specification A detailed, formal problem definition. Often prepared in competitive bidding situations.

Resolution A measure of the precision or sharpness of a graphic image. Often a function of the number of pixels on a screen.

Resource management Managing such resources as processor time, memory space, and peripheral devices. An operating system responsibility.

ROM (read-only memory) A type of memory that cannot be modified by the programmer. Contrast with *RAM*.

Rotational delay On disk or drum, the time required for the desired sector to rotate to the read/write head after the head has been positioned over the desired track.

Routine A program module.

Scheduler An operating system routine that determines which program will be loaded when space becomes available.

Scientific computation Computer applications that support scientific tasks. These applications often call for substantial computation, real-time response, or both.

Second-generation computer An early-1960s computer characterized by transistorized components.

Secondary storage
Nonvolatile memory such as disk or magnetic tape that is used for long-term storage. Generally, the data and instructions that are currently being processed by a computer are stored in main memory; all other data and instructions are stored in secondary storage.

Sector A fixed-length unit of disk or other magnetic storage space that holds a single physical record. A common sector length on microcomputer systems is 512 characters.

Security Activities and controls designed to prevent unauthorized access to a computer system.

Seek time The time needed to position a disk's access mechanism over a specific track.

Sequential access
Accessing records in fixed order, generally the order in which they are physically recorded. Contrast with *Direct access*.

Serial One by one. Serial data transmission involves sending a stream of bits, one after another, over the same wire. Contrast with *Parallel*.

Shell The user interface to an operating system. More generally, the command processor.

Signal degradation The tendency of an electronic signal to lose intensity or die down with distance.

Single-bus architecture A computer architecture in which all internal components are linked by a single bus line.

Slot On a motherboard, one of several openings into which a circuit board can be plugged.

Software Programs and data. Contrast with *Hardware*.

Source code Program instructions written in a source language such as BASIC, COBOL, FORTRAN, or Pascal.

Spooling On input, transferring data to secondary storage and holding them for eventual processing. On output, transferring data to secondary storage for eventual output to an output device.

Spreadsheet, electronic A computer application that simulates an accountant's spreadsheet.

Storage Memory.

Stored program A series of instructions placed in a computer's memory to control that computer. Distinguishes a computer from a calculator.

Supercomputer A powerful, extremely fast computer designed for scientific computation.

System A group of components that function together to achieve an objective. A typical computer-based system contains hardware, software, data, people, and procedures.

System flowchart A graphic representation of a physical system in which symbols represent programs, hardware components, files, and so on.

System software Support software; for example, the operating system. Contrast with *Application program*.

Systems analysis The process of converting a user's needs into technical specifications.

Systems analyst A professional who translates user needs into the technical specifications needed to implement a system.

Telecommunication Transmitting signals over a distance by means of telephone lines, radio signals, or other media.

Terminal Hardware placed at the entry or exit point of a communication network for the purpose of entering or obtaining data.

Third-generation computer A late-1960s and early-1970s computer characterized by integrated circuit components.

Third-generation language A compiler.

Time-sharing A series of techniques that allows multiple users, each controlling an independent terminal, to share a single computer.

Token passing A network management technique in which a signal called a token is passed continuously from terminal to terminal or computer to computer and only the machine that holds the token is allowed to transmit.

Track One of a series of concentric circles around which data are stored on disk or drum. Tracks are often subdivided into sectors.

Transaction An exchange between a user and a computer that accomplishes a single logical function. For example, all the steps involved in requesting cash from an automated teller machine constitute a single transaction.

Transaction processing Processing transactions as they occur rather than in a batch. Contrast with *Batch processing*.

Transmission Sending data from one location to another over a communication line.

User A person or group that uses a program or a system.

User interface The portion of a program that controls communication with the user.

Video disk A secondary storage medium that records and reads data using a laser beam.

Virtual memory A memory management technique in which only active portions of a program are loaded into main memory.

Voice I/O The input or output of spoken sounds.

Volatile memory Memory that loses its content when the power is turned off.

Wait state A condition whereby a given task or process must await the completion of an event before it can resume.

"What if" analysis A type of computer application in which a user makes assumptions and has the computer project the outcome if those assumptions are true. Common in decisions support systems.

Wide area network A network in which the computers are geographically dispersed. Generally, at least some data transmission uses common carriers or public facilities.

Window A portion of the screen that overlays the normal data and allows the user to see an error message, a secondary menu, or even data from a different application.

Word The basic storage unit around which a computer system is designed. On all but the smallest microcomputers a word consists of two or more bytes.

Word processing A computer application that supports the preparation of text.

Workstation A powerful microcomputer, usually with advanced graphics capability. Generally attached to a network.

Index

Index